john

the gospel according to

john

authorised king james version

printed by authority

published by canongate

with an introduction by | blake morrison

First published in Great Britain in 1998
by Canongate Books Ltd
14 High Street, Edinburgh EH1 1TE

10 9 8 7 6 5 4 3 2

Introduction copyright © Blake Morrison 1998
The moral right of the author has been asserted

British Library Cataloguing-in-Publication Data
A catalogue record is available on request from
the British Library

ISBN 0 86241 798 8

Typeset by Palimpsest Book Production
Book design by Paddy Cramsie
Printed and bound in Great Britain
by Caledonian International, Bishopbriggs

a note about pocket canons

The Authorised King James Version of the Bible, translated between 1603–11, coincided with an extraordinary flowering of English literature. This version, more than any other, and possibly more than any other work in history, has had an influence in shaping the language we speak and write today. Presenting individual books from the Bible as separate volumes, as they were originally conceived, encourages the reader to approach them as literary works in their own right.

The first twelve books in this series encompass categories as diverse as history, fiction, philosophy, love poetry and law. Each Pocket Canon also has its own introduction, specially commissioned from an impressive range of writers, which provides a personal interpretation of the text and explores its contemporary relevance.

Blake Morrison was born in Skipton, Yorkshire. He is the author of two collections of poetry, Dark Glasses *and* The Ballad of the Yorkshire Ripper, *and has also written for theatre and television. His best-selling memoir* And when did you last see your father? *won the Waterstone's/Esquire/Volvo Award for Non-Fiction and the J R Ackerley prize for Autobiography in 1993. Most recently, he has published* As If, *which explores the Bulger trial and its aftermath, and* Too True, *a collection of his stories and journalism written over the last five years.*

introduction by blake morrison

From the age of eight to fifteen, I spent every Sunday morning in the choirstalls of an English village church. To be in
the choir didn't require singing talent. You just turned up
each week and stood there, like something out of Thomas
Hardy, raising a song in praise of God, to the accompani-
ment of a wheezing organ. Our predecessors in the grave-
yard had done the same. The dusty black cassocks and white
surplices waiting for us on pegs in the vestry – they had
worn them, too. The choir was small, just six or eight, all
children, most of them present under parental duress. With
me, it was different: my father was an atheist, my mother an
Irish Catholic, and I'd had to fight to join up. It was not that I
had a sense of calling. It was simply a way of getting to see
my friends on Sunday. We weren't always well-behaved.
Gum was surreptitiously chewed during prayers, then depos-
ited in sticky balls and left to harden. Cruel names were
invented for those in the paltry congregation. Whispering
and giggling were routine. Still, until confirmation (which
for me confirmed doubts, not faith) we kept coming. And
though I'm no church-goer now, those Sundays will always
be part of me. The touch of cold stone flags on a bended knee;
the lovely sound of 'daily bread' and 'trespasses'; the melt-
ing nothingness (neither flesh nor manna) of a communion

wafer; the head-swoon from a sip of wine; the rotting-body smell from water that stood too long in flower-vases; the whitewash walls, the spread-winged golden-eagle lectern stand, the pale-lemon morning light, the wood of the nave so dark it might have been burned – the hours of boredom have long faded, but the sensuousness has stayed.

The Gospels have stayed, too, the miracles and sayings and Passion. To begin with, I preferred the Old Testament, which read like a boy's adventure story spanning several generations: Noah's flood, David's slingstone, Daniel in the lion's den, Moses in his basket, the parting of the Red Sea. Jesus had adventures, too, but you'd not have known it from the face in the stained-glass windows. He looked wan, frozen and passive, too pious for his own good – someone who'd change wine to water, not the other way about. The only impressive thing about him was that it had taken four men to tell his tale. Matthew, Mark, Luke and John: the names sounded familiar, reassuring, trustworthy, and it didn't seem surprising that their stories should vary – when my friends and I related the same events, didn't our versions vary, too? As years passed in the choir-stalls, I became more interested in the Apostles, and tried to put faces to their names. John was the hardest to visualise. He was said to be the son of Zebedee, 'the beloved disciple', but this didn't help much. All I did dimly perceive was that he was the odd one out.

At fifteen, I swapped the Apostles for another Fab Four, the Beatles, whose John was likewise the outsider. Soon enough, the phrase 'gospel truth' had a hollow ring for me – I was discovering stranger, more various truths through drink, drugs, girls, music, the mystic east. The only lingering affection I felt for the c of e came from thinking of Jesus's story as myth or legend – literary fiction, not monotheistic truth. The idea that the Apostles were contemporaries of Christ, writing factual first-hand reports, seemed ridiculous. But once I thought of them as storytellers, drawing on oral tradition, their gospels became more interesting. They were pedagogues, trying to convince others to follow their faith. But they were also, at least in the Authorised Version, hauntingly imaginative writers, John above all.

The literary status of the gospels, the identity of their authors, the degree of historical truth they impart – these are matters scholars debate to this day. Agreement is rare, but one can glimpse a consensus of sorts on several points.

— A man called Jesus did live and preach in Palestine shortly after the time of King Herod's death; a radical thinker and militant leader, he ran into trouble with the authorities and was put to death.

— Matthew, Mark, Luke and John wrote their gospels late in the first century, perhaps drawing on eye-witness accounts that had been passed down: their names were assigned to the Gospels only around 180 AD, and they probably worked closely with other Christian opinion-formers, in effect as editorial teams.

— Each gospel went through several versions, perhaps as many as five, building up from sayings and sermons through 'pericopes' (teaching or episodic units) to full-blown narratives.

— Their purpose was to proclaim the 'good news' of Jesus's life, through accounts of his story and teachings: 'these are

blake morrison   ix written, that ye might believe that Jesus is the Christ, the Son of God; and that believing ye might have life through his name' (*John* 20:31).

— *Mark* was the first gospel to be composed and *John* is probably the last.

The apparently late composition of John's gospel is one of several reasons why it's often treated as marginal and inferior. Its resemblance to *Mark* (and *Luke*) suggests that, if not directly dependent on them, it drew on the same sources for episodes such as the walk on the lake, the feeding of the 5,000 and the miraculous draught of fishes. The chronology of the first three ('synoptic') gospels coincides to a very large degree, whereas *John* ('the fourth gospel') differs in suggesting that Jesus's ministry lasted over three Passovers, not one, and in putting the scourging of the Temple episode early on. The synoptic gospels are also fairly consistent about the teachings of Jesus, whereas what he preaches in *John* shows the influence of later schools of thought, including the Hellenistic and the Hermetic. Many commentators find the structure of *John* dislocated and suggest an alternative arrangement of the chapters. All in all, as E P Sanders puts it in his study *The Historical Figure of Jesus*, 'The synoptic gospels are to be preferred as our basic source of information about Jesus.'

What claims can be made for *John*, then? First, it is the most *poetic* of the gospels. Compare the various openings. *Matthew* begins with a dull, Old Testament-like genealogical table: 'Abraham begat Isaac; and Isaac begat Jacob; and Jacob begat Judas', etc. *Mark* goes in for skittish anecdotes and dress-notes about John the Baptist: 'John was clothed with camel's hair, and with a girdle of skin'. *Luke* writes in drab bureaucratese to Theophilus, the recipient of his missive: 'Forasmuch as many have taken in hand to set forth in order a declaration of those things which are most surely believed among us ...' By contrast, *John* opens with one of the greatest passages of poetic prose in the language, philosophically dense, metaphorically rich and rhythmically lucid at the same time:

> In the beginning was the Word, and the Word was with God, and the Word was God. The same was in the beginning with God. All things were made by him; and without him was not any thing made that was made. In him was life; and the life was the light of men. And the light shineth in darkness; and the darkness comprehended it not ... And the Word was made flesh, and dwelt among us (and we beheld his glory, the glory as of the only begotten of the Father), full of grace and truth. (1:1–5, 14)

John is thick with symbols and incantations: light, darkness, bread, water, flesh, word. It's also full of lines that have gone into the language: 'God so loved the world, that he gave his only begotten son ...'; 'Rise, take up thy bed, and walk'; 'He that is without sin among you, let him first cast a stone at her'; 'I am the good shepherd'; 'I am the resurrection, and the life'; 'The poor always ye have with you'; 'In my father's house are many mansions'; 'Greater love hath no man than this, that a man lay down his life for his friends';

'Put up thy sword into thy sheath'; 'What I have written I have written'. Part of what makes John special is that *it uses metaphors where the other Gospels use similes*. 'Destroy this temple,' Jesus tells the Jews, speaking not of their temple but his body, 'and I will raise it up' (2:19). 'Whosoever drinketh of this water shalt thirst again,' he tells the woman of Samaria by her well, 'but whosoever drinketh of the water that I shall give him shall never thirst' (3:13–14). 'I have meat to eat that ye know not of,' he tells his disciples, '… my meat is to do the will of him that sent me' (4:32–4). Or again to his disciples: 'I am the bread of life: he that cometh to me shall never hunger …' (6:35). Or again: 'I am the light of the world' (8:12). Or: 'I am the true vine, and my Father is the husbandman' (15:1).

Metaphors aren't always easy to understand. They trouble the literal-minded. Jesus causes this trouble. One of the themes of John's gospel is *the difficulty people have in communicating with one another*. Jesus's protracted metaphor about entering into a sheepfold leaves his listeners baffled: 'they understood not what things they were which he spake unto them' (10:6). Talk of the impossibility of their following him also causes confusion: 'Then said the Jews, "Will he kill himself?" Because he saith, "Whither I go, ye cannot come."' Nicodemus is perplexed by the promise of rebirth: how *can* a man be reborn, he asks, stirring Jesus into new poetry: 'Marvel not that I said unto thee, "Ye must be born again." The wind bloweth where it listeth, and thou hearest the sound thereof, but canst not tell whence it cometh, and whither it goeth: so is everyone that is born of the Spirit.' *John*'s Jesus is more seer-like than the Jesus of the other gospels: a prophet, an enigma, a stranger from heaven. He is in touch with truths that defy easy comprehension. But he's also self-aware enough to realise his listeners sometimes find him hard-going: 'I have yet many things to say unto you, but ye cannot bear them now.' He doesn't bear listening to in part because he's gnomic. Or if not gnomic, Gnostic. He speaks an alien language, the poetry of God.

John's *characterisation of Jesus* is another reason why this Gospel stands out. Far from being meek and mild, Jesus here is self-assured, pushy, and somewhat dislikeable. It may not have been the author's intention, but we see why he caused such anger and resentment, and understand his enemies' wish to have him dead and out of the way. When he's not speaking in riddles, he's argumentative. He hectors. He harangues. He throws out insults and reproaches. He pulls rank, advertising his credentials as Son of God, Son of Man, Messiah, more divine than human, just passing through: 'Ye are from beneath; I am from above: ye are of this world; I am not of this world (8:23). There is a ferocious existentialist 'I am' about him. Desperate to defeat the doubters, he is not averse to using signs to establish his authority ('Except ye see signs and wonders, ye will not believe'), which the Jesus of Mark's gospel refuses to do, implying it would be a stunt, a piece of cheap magic ('Verily I say unto you, there shall no sign be given unto this generation'). One of the greatest commentators on the fourth gospel, Rudolf Bultmann, has said that 'Jesus as the Revealer of God reveals nothing but that he is the Revealer.' If this makes him sound like some latter-day cultist, prone to mystification and Me-ism, it should also be said that he's robust and resourceful, a cartoon character who keeps getting out of impossible scrapes: 'They took up stones to cast at him: but Jesus hid himself, and went out of the temple, going through the midst of them, and so passed by' (8:59). 'They sought again to take him: but he escaped out of their hand, and went away again beyond Jordan ...' (10:39–40). These escapes continue even after the crucifixion, first when Pilate's soldiers fail to carry out an order to break his legs, then when he disappears from the sepulchre in death as well as life, he constantly outwits his enemies.

The Jesus of John's Apostle is often described as mystic. But *he is worldly as well as otherworldly*. When he scourges the temple moneychangers, it's his physical strength that John emphasises: 'and when he had made a scourge of small cords, he drove them all out of the temple, and the sheep, and the oxen; and poured out the changers' money, and overthrew the tables'. There's more physical immediacy when Jesus spits on the ground, 'and made clay of the spittle', to heal a blind man. And there's Martha's pungent reaction when Jesus proposes to raise her brother Lazarus: 'Lord, by this time he stinketh: for he hath been dead four days.' However high-flown some of the passages in *John*, we never lose sight of fleshly realities. Nor is there any skimping on political realities. Because the ruling powers in Palestine enjoy only limited independence from Rome, they see Jesus as a dangerous rebel, a threat to the status quo: if a popular uprising is sparked by his teaching, 'the Romans shall come and take away both our place and nation' (11:48).

John is also arguably *the most economical of the gospels*: *Mark* is shorter, with 16 chapters to *John*'s 21. But the fourth gospel includes and develops a number of episodes not to be found in the synoptic gospels: for example, the wedding feast at Cana, the raising of Lazarus, and the conversations with Nicodemus and the Woman of Samaria. As a result, its first half, up to Passover, seems to move with extraordinary speed. There is tension from the outset, with the threat to Jesus established as early as chapter 5 ('And therefore did the Jews persecute Jesus and sought to slay him') and the fact that Judas Iscariot will eventually betray him revealed in chapter 6. There's also a feeling of awful inevitability, as in Shakespearian tragedy: beauty and truth are going to pass from the earth because men love darkness rather than light. Despite the prayer and teaching threaded through it, the narrative never slackens in pace. With the crucifixion and resurrection especially, small details do the work of whole paragraphs: the sponge of vinegar put in Christ's mouth, for example, or the empty linen cloths found in his tomb. At the very end, John acknowledges the conciseness of his method: 'And there are also many other things which Jesus did, the which, if they should be written every one, I suppose that even the world itself could not contain the books that should be written.'

This is the kind of sign-off often found in fairytales and fables, gesturing at riches left out. Heresy though it is to say so, the *Gospel of John* has the quality of a fairytale. It has theological and philosophical aspirations too, of course: as one commentator, John Ashton, has put it, 'It is like finding Hans

Christian Andersen hand in hand with Soren Kierkegaard.' But in a secular age, when many people will be left cold by its more didactic passages, the narrative power of the fourth gospel is what redeems it. In Robert Browning's poem 'A Death in the Desert', a dying John foresees a day when readers will ask: 'Was John at all, and did he say he saw?' But whether John was or wasn't, his gospel is not yet redundant. Some will take it as literal truth, and others embrace its imaginative truth. But there's also what Jesus calls 'the truth [that] shall make you free' (8:32). For John, this is what matters most: the possibility that by reading his gospel we will in some way – emotionally, aesthetically, intellectually, spiritually – be liberated.

Liberation wasn't the sensation I got from it as a rustic choirboy. But re-reading it again lately, I felt a story I'd half-forgotten open up again and carry me back to the place where I first heard it. The rhythms of John's gospel can be inspiring and sensuous in that way. He is an enigmatic guide, the odd one out among the Apostles. But he's also a poet through and through.

the gospel according to st john

In the beginning was the Word, and the Word was with God, and the Word was God. ²The same was in the beginning with God. ³All things were made by him; and without him was not any thing made that was made. ⁴In him was life; and the life was the light of men. ⁵And the light shineth in darkness; and the darkness comprehended it not.

⁶There was a man sent from God, whose name was John. ⁷The same came for a witness, to bear witness of the Light, that all men through him might believe. ⁸He was not that Light, but was sent to bear witness of that Light. ⁹That was the true Light, which lighteth every man that cometh into the world. ¹⁰He was in the world, and the world was made by him, and the world knew him not. ¹¹He came unto his own, and his own received him not. ¹²But as many as received him, to them gave he power to become the sons of God, even to them that believe on his name, ¹³which were born, not of blood, nor of the will of the flesh, nor of the will of man, but of God. ¹⁴And the Word was made flesh, and dwelt among us (and we beheld his glory, the glory as of the only begotten of the Father), full of grace and truth.

¹⁵John bare witness of him, and cried, saying, 'This was he of whom I spake, "He that cometh after me is preferred before me, for he was before me."' ¹⁶And of his fulness have

all we received, and grace for grace. ¹⁷ For the law was given by Moses, but grace and truth came by Jesus Christ. ¹⁸ No man hath seen God at any time; the only begotten Son, which is in the bosom of the Father, he hath declared him.

¹⁹ And this is the record of John, when the Jews sent priests and Levites from Jerusalem to ask him, 'Who art thou?' ²⁰ And he confessed, and denied not; but confessed, 'I am not the Christ.' ²¹ And they asked him, 'What then? Art thou Elias?' And he saith, 'I am not.' 'Art thou that prophet?' And he answered, 'No.' ²² Then said they unto him, 'Who art thou? That we may give an answer to them that sent us. What sayest thou of thyself?' ²³ He said, 'I am the voice of one crying in the wilderness, "Make straight the way of the Lord,"' as said the prophet Esaias. ²⁴ And they which were sent were of the Pharisees. ²⁵ And they asked him, and said unto him, 'Why baptizest thou then, if thou be not that Christ, nor Elias, neither that prophet?' ²⁶ John answered them, saying, 'I baptize with water, but there standeth one among you, whom ye know not. ²⁷ He it is, who coming after me is preferred before me, whose shoe's latchet I am not worthy to unloose.' ²⁸ These things were done in Bethabara beyond Jordan, where John was baptizing.

²⁹ The next day John seeth Jesus coming unto him, and saith, 'Behold the Lamb of God, which taketh away the sin of the world. ³⁰ This is he of whom I said, "After me cometh a man which is preferred before me: for he was before me." ³¹ And I knew him not: but that he should be made manifest to Israel, therefore am I come baptizing with water.' ³² And John bare record, saying, 'I saw the Spirit descending from

heaven like a dove, and it abode upon him. ³³And I knew him not: but he that sent me to baptize with water, the same said unto me, "Upon whom thou shalt see the Spirit descending, and remaining on him, the same is he which baptizeth with the Holy Ghost." ³⁴And I saw, and bare record that this is the Son of God.'

³⁵Again the next day after John stood, and two of his disciples; ³⁶and looking upon Jesus as he walked, he saith, 'Behold the Lamb of God!' ³⁷And the two disciples heard him speak, and they followed Jesus. ³⁸Then Jesus turned, and saw them following, and saith unto them, 'What seek ye?' They said unto him, 'Rabbi (which is to say, being interpreted, Master), where dwellest thou?' ³⁹He saith unto them, 'Come and see. They came and saw where he dwelt, and abode with him that day, for it was about the tenth hour.' ⁴⁰One of the two which heard John speak, and followed him, was Andrew, Simon Peter's brother. ⁴¹He first findeth his own brother Simon, and saith unto him, 'We have found the Messias, which is, being interpreted, the Christ.' ⁴²And he brought him to Jesus. And when Jesus beheld him, he said, 'Thou art Simon the son of Jona: thou shalt be called Cephas, which is by interpretation, a stone.'

⁴³The day following Jesus would go forth into Galilee, and findeth Philip, and saith unto him, 'Follow me.' ⁴⁴Now Philip was of Bethsaida, the city of Andrew and Peter. ⁴⁵Philip findeth Nathanael, and saith unto him, 'We have found him, of whom Moses in the law, and the prophets, did write: Jesus of Nazareth, the son of Joseph.' ⁴⁶And Nathanael said unto him, 'Can there any good thing come out of Nazareth?' Philip

saith unto him, 'Come and see.' ⁴⁷ Jesus saw Nathanael coming to him, and saith of him, 'Behold an Israelite indeed, in whom is no guile!' ⁴⁸ Nathanael saith unto him, 'Whence knowest thou me?' Jesus answered and said unto him, 'Before that Philip called thee, when thou wast under the fig tree, I saw thee.' ⁴⁹ Nathanael answered and saith unto him, 'Rabbi, thou art the Son of God; thou art the King of Israel.' ⁵⁰ Jesus answered and said unto him, 'Because I said unto thee, I saw thee under the fig tree, believest thou? Thou shalt see greater things than these.' ⁵¹And he saith unto him, 'Verily, verily, I say unto you, hereafter ye shall see heaven open, and the angels of God ascending and descending upon the Son of man.'

2 And the third day there was a marriage in Cana of Galilee; and the mother of Jesus was there, ² and both Jesus was called, and his disciples, to the marriage. ³ And when they wanted wine, the mother of Jesus saith unto him, 'They have no wine.' ⁴ Jesus saith unto her, 'Woman, what have I to do with thee? Mine hour is not yet come.' ⁵ His mother saith unto the servants, 'Whatsoever he saith unto you, do it.' ⁶And there were set there six waterpots of stone, after the manner of the purifying of the Jews, containing two or three firkins apiece. ⁷ Jesus saith unto them, 'Fill the waterpots with water.' And they filled them up to the brim. ⁸And he saith unto them, 'Draw out now, and bear unto the governor of the feast.' And they bare it. ⁹ When the ruler of the feast had tasted the water that was made wine, and knew not whence it was (but the servants which drew the water knew), the governor of the feast called the bridegroom, ¹⁰ and saith

unto him, 'Every man at the beginning doth set forth good wine; and when men have well drunk, then that which is worse: but thou hast kept the good wine until now.' ¹¹This beginning of miracles did Jesus in Cana of Galilee, and manifested forth his glory; and his disciples believed on him.

¹²After this he went down to Capernaum, he, and his mother, and his brethren, and his disciples, and they continued there not many days.

¹³And the Jews' passover was at hand, and Jesus went up to Jerusalem, ¹⁴and found in the temple those that sold oxen and sheep and doves, and the changers of money sitting: ¹⁵and when he had made a scourge of small cords, he drove them all out of the temple, and the sheep, and the oxen; and poured out the changers' money, and overthrew the tables; ¹⁶and said unto them that sold doves, 'Take these things hence; make not my Father's house an house of merchandise.' ¹⁷And his disciples remembered that it was written, 'The zeal of thine house hath eaten me up.'

¹⁸Then answered the Jews and said unto him, 'What sign shewest thou unto us, seeing that thou doest these things?' ¹⁹Jesus answered and said unto them, 'Destroy this temple, and in three days I will raise it up.' ²⁰Then said the Jews, 'Forty and six years was this temple in building, and wilt thou rear it up in three days?' ²¹But he spake of the temple of his body. ²²When therefore he was risen from the dead, his disciples remembered that he had said this unto them; and they believed the scripture, and the word which Jesus had said.

²³Now when he was in Jerusalem at the passover, in the feast day, many believed in his name, when they saw the

miracles which he did. ²⁴But Jesus did not commit himself unto them, because he knew all men, ²⁵and needed not that any should testify of man, for he knew what was in man.

3 There was a man of the Pharisees, named Nicodemus, a ruler of the Jews. ²The same came to Jesus by night, and said unto him, 'Rabbi, we know that thou art a teacher come from God, for no man can do these miracles that thou doest, except God be with him.' ³Jesus answered and said unto him, 'Verily, verily, I say unto thee, except a man be born again, he cannot see the kingdom of God.' ⁴Nicodemus saith unto him, 'How can a man be born when he is old? Can he enter the second time into his mother's womb, and be born?' ⁵Jesus answered, 'Verily, verily, I say unto thee, except a man be born of water and of the Spirit, he cannot enter into the kingdom of God. ⁶That which is born of the flesh is flesh; and that which is born of the Spirit is spirit. ⁷Marvel not that I said unto thee, ye must be born again.' ⁸The wind bloweth where it listeth, and thou hearest the sound thereof, but canst not tell whence it cometh, and whither it goeth: so is every one that is born of the Spirit.' ⁹Nicodemus answered and said unto him, 'How can these things be?' ¹⁰Jesus answered and said unto him, 'Art thou a master of Israel, and knowest not these things? ¹¹Verily, verily, I say unto thee, we speak that we do know, and testify that we have seen; and ye receive not our witness. ¹²If I have told you earthly things, and ye believe not, how shall ye believe, if I tell you of heavenly things? ¹³And no man hath ascended up to heaven, but he that came down from heaven, even the Son of man which is in heaven.

¹⁴ 'And as Moses lifted up the serpent in the wilderness, even so must the Son of man be lifted up: ¹⁵ that whosoever believeth in him should not perish, but have eternal life.

¹⁶ 'For God so loved the world, that he gave his only begotten Son, that whosoever believeth in him should not perish, but have everlasting life. ¹⁷ For God sent not his Son into the world to condemn the world; but that the world through him might be saved.

¹⁸ 'He that believeth on him is not condemned: but he that believeth not is condemned already, because he hath not believed in the name of the only begotten Son of God. ¹⁹ And this is the condemnation, that light is come into the world, and men loved darkness rather than light, because their deeds were evil. ²⁰ For every one that doeth evil hateth the light, neither cometh to the light, lest his deeds should be reproved. ²¹ But he that doeth truth cometh to the light, that his deeds may be made manifest, that they are wrought in God.'

²² After these things came Jesus and his disciples into the land of Judæa; and there he tarried with them, and baptized.

²³ And John also was baptizing in Ænon near to Salim, because there was much water there, and they came, and were baptized. ²⁴ For John was not yet cast into prison.

²⁵ Then there arose a question between some of John's disciples and the Jews about purifying. ²⁶ And they came unto John, and said unto him, 'Rabbi, he that was with thee beyond Jordan, to whom thou barest witness, behold, the same baptizeth, and all men come to him.' ²⁷ John answered and said, 'A man can receive nothing, except it be given him from heaven. ²⁸ Ye yourselves bear me witness, that I said, "I am

not the Christ," but that I am sent before him. ²⁹ He that hath the bride is the bridegroom, but the friend of the bridegroom, which standeth and heareth him, rejoiceth greatly because of the bridegroom's voice: this my joy therefore is fulfilled. ³⁰ He must increase, but I must decrease. ³¹ He that cometh from above is above all; he that is of the earth is earthly, and speaketh of the earth; he that cometh from heaven is above all. ³² And what he hath seen and heard, that he testifieth; and no man receiveth his testimony. ³³ He that hath received his testimony hath set to his seal that God is true. ³⁴ For he whom God hath sent speaketh the words of God, for God giveth not the Spirit by measure unto him. ³⁵ The Father loveth the Son, and hath given all things into his hand. ³⁶ He that believeth on the Son hath everlasting life, and he that believeth not the Son shall not see life; but the wrath of God abideth on him.'

4 When therefore the Lord knew how the Pharisees had heard that Jesus made and baptized more disciples than John ²(though Jesus himself baptized not, but his disciples), ³ he left Judæa, and departed again into Galilee. ⁴ And he must needs go through Samaria. ⁵ Then cometh he to a city of Samaria, which is called Sychar, near to the parcel of ground that Jacob gave to his son Joseph. ⁶ Now Jacob's well was there. Jesus therefore, being wearied with his journey, sat thus on the well, and it was about the sixth hour. ⁷ There cometh a woman of Samaria to draw water. Jesus saith unto her, 'Give me to drink.' ⁸(For his disciples were gone away unto the city to buy meat.) ⁹ Then saith the woman of Samaria unto him,

'How is it that thou, being a Jew, askest drink of me, which am a woman of Samaria?' For the Jews have no dealings with the Samaritans. [10] Jesus answered and said unto her, 'If thou knewest the gift of God, and who it is that saith to thee, "Give me to drink," thou wouldest have asked of him, and he would have given thee living water.' [11] The woman saith unto him, 'Sir, thou hast nothing to draw with, and the well is deep; from whence then hast thou that living water? [12] Art thou greater than our father Jacob, which gave us the well, and drank thereof himself, and his children, and his cattle?' [13] Jesus answered and said unto her, 'Whosoever drinketh of this water shall thirst again: [14] but whosoever drinketh of the water that I shall give him shall never thirst; but the water that I shall give him shall be in him a well of water springing up into everlasting life.' [15] The woman saith unto him, 'Sir, give me this water, that I thirst not, neither come hither to draw.' [16] Jesus saith unto her, 'Go, call thy husband, and come hither.' [17] The woman answered and said, 'I have no husband.' Jesus said unto her, 'Thou hast well said, "I have no husband," [18] for thou hast had five husbands; and he whom thou now hast is not thy husband; in that saidst thou truly.' [19] The woman saith unto him, 'Sir, I perceive that thou art a prophet. [20] Our fathers worshipped in this mountain; and ye say, that in Jerusalem is the place where men ought to worship.' [21] Jesus saith unto her, 'Woman, believe me, the hour cometh, when ye shall neither in this mountain, nor yet at Jerusalem, worship the Father. [22] Ye worship ye know not what: we know what we worship, for salvation is of the Jews. [23] But the hour cometh, and now is, when the true worshippers shall worship the Father in spirit and in truth, for the Father seeketh such to worship him. [24] God is a Spirit, and they that worship him must worship him in spirit and in truth.' [25] The woman saith unto him, 'I know that Messias cometh, which is called Christ: when he is come, he will tell us all things.' [26] Jesus saith unto her, 'I that speak unto thee am he.'

[27] And upon this came his disciples, and marvelled that he talked with the woman; yet no man said, 'What seekest thou?' or 'Why talkest thou with her?' [28] The woman then left her waterpot, and went her way into the city, and saith to the men, [29] 'Come, see a man, which told me all things that ever I did: is not this the Christ?' [30] Then they went out of the city, and came unto him.

[31] In the mean while his disciples prayed him, saying, 'Master, eat.' [32] But he said unto them, 'I have meat to eat that ye know not of.' [33] Therefore said the disciples one to another, 'Hath any man brought him ought to eat?' [34] Jesus saith unto them, 'My meat is to do the will of him that sent me, and to finish his work. [35] Say not ye, "There are yet four months, and then cometh harvest"? Behold, I say unto you, lift up your eyes, and look on the fields: for they are white already to harvest. [36] And he that reapeth receiveth wages, and gathereth fruit unto life eternal, that both he that soweth and he that reapeth may rejoice together. [37] And herein is that saying true, "One soweth, and another reapeth." [38] I sent you to reap that whereon ye bestowed no labour; other men laboured, and ye are entered into their labours.'

[39] And many of the Samaritans of that city believed on him for the saying of the woman, which testified, 'He told

me all that ever I did.' ⁴⁰ So when the Samaritans were come unto him, they besought him that he would tarry with them, and he abode there two days. ⁴¹ And many more believed because of his own word; ⁴² and said unto the woman, 'Now we believe, not because of thy saying, for we have heard him ourselves, and know that this is indeed the Christ, the Saviour of the world.'

⁴³ Now after two days he departed thence, and went into Galilee. ⁴⁴ For Jesus himself testified that a prophet hath no honour in his own country. ⁴⁵ Then when he was come into Galilee, the Galilæans received him, having seen all the things that he did at Jerusalem at the feast, for they also went unto the feast. ⁴⁶ So Jesus came again into Cana of Galilee, where he made the water wine. And there was a certain nobleman, whose son was sick at Capernaum. ⁴⁷ When he heard that Jesus was come out of Judæa into Galilee, he went unto him, and besought him that he would come down, and heal his son, for he was at the point of death. ⁴⁸ Then said Jesus unto him, 'Except ye see signs and wonders, ye will not believe.' ⁴⁹ The nobleman saith unto him, 'Sir, come down ere my child die.' ⁵⁰ Jesus saith unto him, 'Go thy way; thy son liveth.' And the man believed the word that Jesus had spoken unto him, and he went his way. ⁵¹ And as he was now going down, his servants met him, and told him, saying, 'Thy son liveth.' ⁵² Then enquired he of them the hour when he began to amend. And they said unto him, 'Yesterday at the seventh hour the fever left him.' ⁵³ So the father knew that it was at the same hour, in the which Jesus said unto him, 'Thy son liveth,' and himself believed, and his

whole house. ⁵⁴ This is again the second miracle that Jesus did, when he was come out of Judæa into Galilee.

5 After this there was a feast of the Jews; and Jesus went up to Jerusalem. ² Now there is at Jerusalem by the sheep market a pool, which is called in the Hebrew tongue Bethesda, having five porches. ³ In these lay a great multitude of impotent folk, of blind, halt, withered, waiting for the moving of the water. ⁴ For an angel went down at a certain season into the pool, and troubled the water: whosoever then first after the troubling of the water stepped in was made whole of whatsoever disease he had. ⁵ And a certain man was there, which had an infirmity thirty and eight years. ⁶ When Jesus saw him lie, and knew that he had been now a long time in that case, he saith unto him, 'Wilt thou be made whole?' ⁷ The impotent man answered him, 'Sir, I have no man, when the water is troubled, to put me into the pool: but while I am coming, another steppeth down before me.' ⁸ Jesus saith unto him, 'Rise, take up thy bed, and walk.' ⁹ And immediately the man was made whole, and took up his bed, and walked; and on the same day was the sabbath.

¹⁰ The Jews therefore said unto him that was cured, 'It is the sabbath day: it is not lawful for thee to carry thy bed.' ¹¹ He answered them, 'He that made me whole, the same said unto me, "Take up thy bed, and walk."' ¹² Then asked they him, 'What man is that which said unto thee, "Take up thy bed, and walk?"' ¹³ And he that was healed wist not who it was, for Jesus had conveyed himself away, a multitude being in that place. ¹⁴ Afterward Jesus findeth him in the temple,

and said unto him, 'Behold, thou art made whole; sin no more, lest a worse thing come unto thee.' [15] The man departed, and told the Jews that it was Jesus, which had made him whole. [16] And therefore did the Jews persecute Jesus, and sought to slay him, because he had done these things on the sabbath day.

[17] But Jesus answered them, 'My Father worketh hitherto, and I work.' [18] Therefore the Jews sought the more to kill him, because he not only had broken the sabbath, but said also that God was his Father, making himself equal with God. [19] Then answered Jesus and said unto them, 'Verily, verily, I say unto you, the Son can do nothing of himself, but what he seeth the Father do: for what things soever he doeth, these also doeth the Son likewise. [20] For the Father loveth the Son, and sheweth him all things that himself doeth, and he will shew him greater works than these, that ye may marvel. [21] For as the Father raiseth up the dead, and quickeneth them; even so the Son quickeneth whom he will. [22] For the Father judgeth no man, but hath committed all judgment unto the Son, [23] that all men should honour the Son, even as they honour the Father. He that honoureth not the Son honoureth not the Father which hath sent him. [24] Verily, verily, I say unto you, he that heareth my word, and believeth on him that sent me, hath everlasting life, and shall not come into condemnation; but is passed from death unto life. [25] Verily, verily, I say unto you, the hour is coming, and now is, when the dead shall hear the voice of the Son of God, and they that hear shall live. [26] For as the Father hath life in himself; so hath he given to the Son to have life in himself; [27] and hath

given him authority to execute judgment also, because he is the Son of man. ²⁸Marvel not at this, for the hour is coming, in the which all that are in the graves shall hear his voice, ²⁹and shall come forth; they that have done good, unto the resurrection of life; and they that have done evil, unto the resurrection of damnation. ³⁰I can of mine own self do nothing: as I hear, I judge, and my judgment is just; because I seek not mine own will, but the will of the Father which hath sent me. ³¹If I bear witness of myself, my witness is not true.

³²'There is another that beareth witness of me; and I know that the witness which he witnesseth of me is true. ³³Ye sent unto John, and he bare witness unto the truth. ³⁴But I receive not testimony from man: but these things I say, that ye might be saved. ³⁵He was a burning and a shining light, and ye were willing for a season to rejoice in his light.

³⁶'But I have greater witness than that of John: for the works which the Father hath given me to finish, the same works that I do, bear witness of me, that the Father hath sent me. ³⁷And the Father himself, which hath sent me, hath borne witness of me. Ye have neither heard his voice at any time, nor seen his shape. ³⁸And ye have not his word abiding in you: for whom he hath sent, him ye believe not.

³⁹'Search the scriptures, for in them ye think ye have eternal life: and they are they which testify of me. ⁴⁰And ye will not come to me, that ye might have life. ⁴¹I receive not honour from men. ⁴²But I know you, that ye have not the love of God in you. ⁴³I am come in my Father's name, and ye receive me not; if another shall come in his own name, him ye will receive. ⁴⁴How can ye believe, which receive honour one of

another, and seek not the honour that cometh from God only? [45] Do not think that I will accuse you to the Father: there is one that accuseth you, even Moses, in whom ye trust. [46] For had ye believed Moses, ye would have believed me: for he wrote of me. [47] But if ye believe not his writings, how shall ye believe my words?'

6 After these things Jesus went over the sea of Galilee, which is the sea of Tiberias. [2] And a great multitude followed him, because they saw his miracles which he did on them that were diseased. [3] And Jesus went up into a mountain, and there he sat with his disciples. [4] And the passover, a feast of the Jews, was nigh.

[5] When Jesus then lifted up his eyes, and saw a great company come unto him, he saith unto Philip, 'Whence shall we buy bread, that these may eat?' [6] And this he said to prove him, for he himself knew what he would do. [7] Philip answered him, 'Two hundred pennyworth of bread is not sufficient for them, that every one of them may take a little.' [8] One of his disciples, Andrew, Simon Peter's brother, saith unto him, [9] 'There is a lad here, which hath five barley loaves, and two small fishes, but what are they among so many?' [10] And Jesus said, 'Make the men sit down.' Now there was much grass in the place. So the men sat down, in number about five thousand. [11] And Jesus took the loaves; and when he had given thanks, he distributed to the disciples, and the disciples to them that were set down; and likewise of the fishes as much as they would. [12] When they were filled, he said unto his disciples, 'Gather up the fragments that remain, that nothing be

lost.' ¹³ Therefore they gathered them together, and filled twelve baskets with the fragments of the five barley loaves, which remained over and above unto them that had eaten. ¹⁴ Then those men, when they had seen the miracle that Jesus did, said, 'This is of a truth that prophet that should come into the world.'

¹⁵ When Jesus therefore perceived that they would come and take him by force, to make him a king, he departed again into a mountain himself alone. ¹⁶ And when even was now come, his disciples went down unto the sea, ¹⁷ and entered into a ship, and went over the sea toward Capernaum. And it was now dark, and Jesus was not come to them. ¹⁸ And the sea arose by reason of a great wind that blew. ¹⁹ So when they had rowed about five and twenty or thirty furlongs, they see Jesus walking on the sea, and drawing nigh unto the ship, and they were afraid. ²⁰ But he saith unto them, 'It is I; be not afraid.' ²¹ Then they willingly received him into the ship, and immediately the ship was at the land whither they went.

²² The day following, when the people which stood on the other side of the sea saw that there was none other boat there, save that one whereinto his disciples were entered, and that Jesus went not with his disciples into the boat, but that his disciples were gone away alone. ²³ (Howbeit there came other boats from Tiberias nigh unto the place where they did eat bread, after that the Lord had given thanks.) ²⁴ When the people therefore saw that Jesus was not there, neither his disciples, they also took shipping, and came to Capernaum, seeking for Jesus. ²⁵ And when they had found him on the other side of the sea, they said unto him, 'Rabbi,

when camest thou hither?' ²⁶ Jesus answered them and said, 'Verily, verily, I say unto you, ye seek me, not because ye saw the miracles, but because ye did eat of the loaves, and were filled. ²⁷ Labour not for the meat which perisheth, but for that meat which endureth unto everlasting life, which the Son of man shall give unto you: for him hath God the Father sealed.' ²⁸ Then said they unto him, 'What shall we do, that we might work the works of God?' ²⁹ Jesus answered and said unto them, 'This is the work of God, that ye believe on him whom he hath sent.' ³⁰ They said therefore unto him, 'What sign shewest thou then, that we may see, and believe thee? What dost thou work? ³¹ Our fathers did eat manna in the desert; as it is written, "He gave them bread from heaven to eat."' ³² Then Jesus said unto them, 'Verily, verily, I say unto you, Moses gave you not that bread from heaven; but my Father giveth you the true bread from heaven. ³³ For the bread of God is he which cometh down from heaven, and giveth life unto the world.' ³⁴ Then said they unto him, 'Lord, evermore give us this bread.' ³⁵ And Jesus said unto them, 'I am the bread of life: he that cometh to me shall never hunger; and he that believeth on me shall never thirst. ³⁶ But I said unto you that ye also have seen me, and believe not. ³⁷ All that the Father giveth me shall come to me; and him that cometh to me I will in no wise cast out. ³⁸ For I came down from heaven, not to do mine own will, but the will of him that sent me. ³⁹ And this is the Father's will which hath sent me: that of all which he hath given me I should lose nothing, but should raise it up again at the last day. ⁴⁰ And this is the will of him that sent me: that every one which seeth the Son, and believeth on him, may have everlasting life, and I will raise him up at the last day.' [41] The Jews then murmured at him, because he said, 'I am the bread which came down from heaven.' [42] And they said, 'Is not this Jesus, the son of Joseph, whose father and mother we know? How is it then that he saith, "I came down from heaven"?' [43] Jesus therefore answered and said unto them, 'Murmur not among yourselves. [44] No man can come to me, except the Father which hath sent me draw him, and I will raise him up at the last day. [45] It is written in the prophets, "And they shall be all taught of God." Every man therefore that hath heard, and hath learned of the Father, cometh unto me. [46] Not that any man hath seen the Father, save he which is of God, he hath seen the Father. [47] Verily, verily, I say unto you, he that believeth on me hath everlasting life. [48] I am that bread of life. [49] Your fathers did eat manna in the wilderness, and are dead. [50] This is the bread which cometh down from heaven, that a man may eat thereof, and not die. [51] I am the living bread which came down from heaven: if any man eat of this bread, he shall live for ever; and the bread that I will give is my flesh, which I will give for the life of the world.' [52] The Jews therefore strove among themselves, saying, 'How can this man give us his flesh to eat?' [53] Then Jesus said unto them, 'Verily, verily, I say unto you, except ye eat the flesh of the Son of man, and drink his blood, ye have no life in you. [54] Whoso eateth my flesh, and drinketh my blood, hath eternal life; and I will raise him up at the last day. [55] For my flesh is meat indeed, and my blood is drink indeed. [56] He that eateth my flesh, and drinketh my blood, dwelleth in me, and I in him. [57] As the living Father hath sent me, and I live by the Father, so he that eateth me, even he shall live by me. ⁵⁸ This is that bread which came down from heaven: not as your fathers did eat manna, and are dead. He that eateth of this bread shall live for ever.' ⁵⁹ These things said he in the synagogue, as he taught in Capernaum. ⁶⁰ Many therefore of his disciples, when they had heard this, said, 'This is an hard saying; who can hear it?' ⁶¹ When Jesus knew in himself that his disciples murmured at it, he said unto them, 'Doth this offend you? ⁶² What and if ye shall see the Son of man ascend up where he was before? ⁶³ It is the spirit that quickeneth; the flesh profiteth nothing; the words that I speak unto you, they are spirit, and they are life. ⁶⁴ But there are some of you that believe not.' For Jesus knew from the beginning who they were that believed not, and who should betray him. ⁶⁵ And he said, 'Therefore said I unto you, that no man can come unto me, except it were given unto him of my Father.'

⁶⁶ From that time many of his disciples went back, and walked no more with him. ⁶⁷ Then said Jesus unto the twelve, 'Will ye also go away?' ⁶⁸ Then Simon Peter answered him, 'Lord, to whom shall we go? Thou hast the words of eternal life. ⁶⁹ And we believe and are sure that thou art that Christ, the Son of the living God.' ⁷⁰ Jesus answered them, 'Have not I chosen you twelve, and one of you is a devil?' ⁷¹ He spake of Judas Iscariot the son of Simon: for he it was that should betray him, being one of the twelve.

7 After these things Jesus walked in Galilee: for he would not walk in Jewry, because the Jews sought to kill him.

²Now the Jews' feast of tabernacles was at hand. ³His brethren therefore said unto him, 'Depart hence, and go into Judæa, that thy disciples also may see the works that thou doest. ⁴For there is no man that doeth any thing in secret, and he himself seeketh to be known openly. If thou do these things, shew thyself to the world.' ⁵For neither did his brethren believe in him. ⁶Then Jesus said unto them, 'My time is not yet come, but your time is alway ready. ⁷The world cannot hate you; but me it hateth, because I testify of it, that the works thereof are evil. ⁸Go ye up unto this feast. I go not up yet unto this feast; for my time is not yet full come.' ⁹When he had said these words unto them, he abode still in Galilee.

¹⁰But when his brethren were gone up, then went he also up unto the feast, not openly, but as it were in secret. ¹¹Then the Jews sought him at the feast, and said, 'Where is he?' ¹²And there was much murmuring among the people concerning him, for some said, 'He is a good man,' others said, 'Nay; but he deceiveth the people.' ¹³Howbeit no man spake openly of him for fear of the Jews.

¹⁴Now about the midst of the feast Jesus went up into the temple, and taught. ¹⁵And the Jews marvelled, saying, 'How knoweth this man letters, having never learned?' ¹⁶Jesus answered them, and said, 'My doctrine is not mine, but his that sent me. ¹⁷If any man will do his will, he shall know of the doctrine, whether it be of God, or whether I speak of myself. ¹⁸He that speaketh of himself seeketh his own glory: but he that seeketh his glory that sent him, the same is true, and no unrighteousness is in him. ¹⁹Did not Moses give you the law, and yet none of you keepeth the law? Why go ye

about to kill me?' ²⁰ The people answered and said, 'Thou hast a devil. Who goeth about to kill thee?' ²¹ Jesus answered and said unto them, 'I have done one work, and ye all marvel. ²² Moses therefore gave unto you circumcision (not because it is of Moses, but of the fathers), and ye on the sabbath day circumcise a man. ²³ If a man on the sabbath day receive circumcision, that the law of Moses should not be broken; are ye angry at me, because I have made a man every whit whole on the sabbath day? ²⁴ Judge not according to the appearance, but judge righteous judgment.' ²⁵ Then said some of them of Jerusalem, 'Is not this he, whom they seek to kill? ²⁶ But, lo, he speaketh boldly, and they say nothing unto him. Do the rulers know indeed that this is the very Christ? ²⁷ Howbeit we know this man whence he is, but when Christ cometh, no man knoweth whence he is.' ²⁸ Then cried Jesus in the temple as he taught, saying, 'Ye both know me, and ye know whence I am; and I am not come of myself, but he that sent me is true, whom ye know not. ²⁹ But I know him, for I am from him, and he hath sent me.' ³⁰ Then they sought to take him: but no man laid hands on him, because his hour was not yet come. ³¹ And many of the people believed on him, and said, 'When Christ cometh, will he do more miracles than these which this man hath done?'

³² The Pharisees heard that the people murmured such things concerning him; and the Pharisees and the chief priests sent officers to take him. ³³ Then said Jesus unto them, 'Yet a little while am I with you, and then I go unto him that sent me. ³⁴ Ye shall seek me, and shall not find me, and where I am, thither ye cannot come.' ³⁵ Then said the Jews among

themselves, 'Whither will he go, that we shall not find him? Will he go unto the dispersed among the Gentiles, and teach the Gentiles? ³⁶ What manner of saying is this that he said, "Ye shall seek me, and shall not find me, and where I am, thither ye cannot come"?' ³⁷ In the last day, that great day of the feast, Jesus stood and cried, saying, 'If any man thirst, let him come unto me, and drink. ³⁸ He that believeth on me, as the scripture hath said, out of his belly shall flow rivers of living water.' ³⁹(But this spake he of the Spirit, which they that believe on him should receive: for the Holy Ghost was not yet given; because that Jesus was not yet glorified.)

⁴⁰ Many of the people therefore, when they heard this saying, said, 'Of a truth this is the Prophet.' ⁴¹ Others said, 'This is the Christ.' But some said, 'Shall Christ come out of Galilee? ⁴² Hath not the scripture said that Christ cometh of the seed of David, and out of the town of Bethlehem, where David was?' ⁴³ So there was a division among the people because of him. ⁴⁴ And some of them would have taken him; but no man laid hands on him.

⁴⁵ Then came the officers to the chief priests and Pharisees; and they said unto them, 'Why have ye not brought him?' ⁴⁶ The officers answered, 'Never man spake like this man.' ⁴⁷ Then answered them the Pharisees, 'Are ye also deceived? ⁴⁸ Have any of the rulers or of the Pharisees believed on him? ⁴⁹ But this people who knoweth not the law are cursed.' ⁵⁰ Nicodemus saith unto them (he that came to Jesus by night, being one of them), ⁵¹ 'Doth our law judge any man, before it hear him, and know what he doeth?' ⁵² They answered and said unto him, 'Art thou also of Galilee? Search, and look: for

out of Galilee ariseth no prophet.' ⁵³And every man went
unto his own house.

8 Jesus went unto the mount of Olives. ²And early in the
morning he came again into the temple, and all the people
came unto him; and he sat down, and taught them. ³And the
scribes and Pharisees brought unto him a woman taken in
adultery; and when they had set her in the midst, ⁴they say
unto him, 'Master, this woman was taken in adultery, in the
very act. ⁵Now Moses in the law commanded us, that such
should be stoned, but what sayest thou?' ⁶This they said,
tempting him, that they might have to accuse him. But Jesus
stooped down, and with his finger wrote on the ground, as
though he heard them not. ⁷So when they continued asking
him, he lifted up himself, and said unto them, 'He that is
without sin among you, let him first cast a stone at her.' ⁸And
again he stooped down, and wrote on the ground. ⁹And they
which heard it, being convicted by their own conscience, went
out one by one, beginning at the eldest, even unto the last,
and Jesus was left alone, and the woman standing in the
midst. ¹⁰When Jesus had lifted up himself, and saw none but
the woman, he said unto her, 'Woman, where are those thine
accusers? Hath no man condemned thee?' ¹¹She said, 'No man,
Lord.' And Jesus said unto her, 'Neither do I condemn thee:
go, and sin no more.'

¹²Then spake Jesus again unto them, saying, 'I am the
light of the world: he that followeth me shall not walk in
darkness, but shall have the light of life.' ¹³The Pharisees
therefore said unto him, 'Thou bearest record of thyself; thy

record is not true.' ¹⁴ Jesus answered and said unto them, 'Though I bear record of myself, yet my record is true, for I know whence I came, and whither I go; but ye cannot tell whence I come, and whither I go. ¹⁵ Ye judge after the flesh; I judge no man. ¹⁶ And yet if I judge, my judgment is true, for I am not alone, but I and the Father that sent me. ¹⁷ It is also written in your law, that the testimony of two men is true. ¹⁸ I am one that bear witness of myself, and the Father that sent me beareth witness of me.' ¹⁹ Then said they unto him, 'Where is thy Father?' Jesus answered, 'Ye neither know me, nor my Father. If ye had known me, ye should have known my Father also.' ²⁰ These words spake Jesus in the treasury, as he taught in the temple, and no man laid hands on him; for his hour was not yet come. ²¹ Then said Jesus again unto them, 'I go my way, and ye shall seek me, and shall die in your sins. Whither I go, ye cannot come.' ²² Then said the Jews, 'Will he kill himself?' because he saith, 'Whither I go, ye cannot come.' ²³ And he said unto them, 'Ye are from beneath; I am from above: ye are of this world; I am not of this world. ²⁴ I said therefore unto you, that ye shall die in your sins: for if ye believe not that I am he, ye shall die in your sins.' ²⁵ Then said they unto him, 'Who art thou?' And Jesus saith unto them, 'Even the same that I said unto you from the beginning. ²⁶ I have many things to say and to judge of you, but he that sent me is true; and I speak to the world those things which I have heard of him.' ²⁷ They understood not that he spake to them of the Father. ²⁸ Then said Jesus unto them, 'When ye have lifted up the Son of man, then shall ye know that I am he, and that I do nothing of myself; but as my Father hath taught me, I speak these things. ²⁹And he that sent me is with me: the Father hath not left me alone, for I do always those things that please him.' ³⁰As he spake these words, many believed on him. ³¹Then said Jesus to those Jews which believed on him, 'If ye continue in my word, then are ye my disciples indeed; ³²and ye shall know the truth, and the truth shall make you free.'

³³They answered him, 'We be Abraham's seed, and were never in bondage to any man. How sayest thou, "Ye shall be made free"?' ³⁴Jesus answered them, 'Verily, verily, I say unto you, whosoever committeth sin is the servant of sin. ³⁵And the servant abideth not in the house for ever, but the Son abideth ever. ³⁶If the Son therefore shall make you free, ye shall be free indeed. ³⁷I know that ye are Abraham's seed; but ye seek to kill me, because my word hath no place in you. ³⁸I speak that which I have seen with my Father, and ye do that which ye have seen with your father.' ³⁹They answered and said unto him, 'Abraham is our father.' Jesus saith unto them, 'If ye were Abraham's children, ye would do the works of Abraham. ⁴⁰But now ye seek to kill me, a man that hath told you the truth, which I have heard of God: this did not Abraham. ⁴¹Ye do the deeds of your father.' Then said they to him, 'We be not born of fornication; we have one Father, even God.' ⁴²Jesus said unto them, 'If God were your Father, ye would love me: for I proceeded forth and came from God; neither came I of myself, but he sent me. ⁴³Why do ye not understand my speech? Even because ye cannot hear my word. ⁴⁴Ye are of your father the devil, and the lusts of your father ye will do. He was a murderer from the beginning,

and abode not in the truth, because there is no truth in him. When he speaketh a lie, he speaketh of his own: for he is a liar, and the father of it. ⁴⁵And because I tell you the truth, ye believe me not. ⁴⁶Which of you convinceth me of sin? And if I say the truth, why do ye not believe me? ⁴⁷He that is of God heareth God's words: ye therefore hear them not, because ye are not of God.' ⁴⁸Then answered the Jews, and said unto him, 'Say we not well that thou art a Samaritan, and hast a devil?' ⁴⁹Jesus answered, 'I have not a devil; but I honour my Father, and ye do dishonour me. ⁵⁰And I seek not mine own glory: there is one that seeketh and judgeth. ⁵¹Verily, verily, I say unto you, if a man keep my saying, he shall never see death.' ⁵²Then said the Jews unto him, 'Now we know that thou hast a devil. Abraham is dead, and the prophets; and thou sayest, "If a man keep my saying, he shall never taste of death." ⁵³Art thou greater than our father Abraham, which is dead? And the prophets are dead. Whom makest thou thyself?' ⁵⁴Jesus answered, 'If I honour myself, my honour is nothing: it is my Father that honoureth me; of whom ye say, that he is your God; ⁵⁵yet ye have not known him; but I know him, and if I should say, "I know him not" I shall be a liar like unto you; but I know him, and keep his saying. ⁵⁶Your father Abraham rejoiced to see my day, and he saw it, and was glad.' ⁵⁷Then said the Jews unto him, 'Thou art not yet fifty years old, and hast thou seen Abraham?' ⁵⁸Jesus said unto them, 'Verily, verily, I say unto you, before Abraham was, I am.' ⁵⁹Then took they up stones to cast at him: but Jesus hid himself, and went out of the temple, going through the midst of them, and so passed by.

9 And as Jesus passed by, he saw a man which was blind from his birth. ²And his disciples asked him, saying, 'Master, who did sin, this man, or his parents, that he was born blind?' ³Jesus answered, 'Neither hath this man sinned, nor his parents, but that the works of God should be made manifest in him. ⁴I must work the works of him that sent me, while it is day; the night cometh, when no man can work. ⁵As long as I am in the world, I am the light of the world.' ⁶When he had thus spoken, he spat on the ground, and made clay of the spittle, and he anointed the eyes of the blind man with the clay, ⁷and said unto him, 'Go, wash in the pool of Siloam' (which is by interpretation, Sent). He went his way therefore, and washed, and came seeing.

⁸The neighbours therefore, and they which before had seen him that he was blind, said, 'Is not this he that sat and begged?' ⁹Some said, 'This is he,' others said, 'He is like him,' but he said, 'I am he.' ¹⁰Therefore said they unto him, 'How were thine eyes opened?' ¹¹He answered and said, 'A man that is called Jesus made clay, and anointed mine eyes, and said unto me, "Go to the pool of Siloam, and wash," and I went and washed, and I received sight.' ¹²Then said they unto him, 'Where is he?' He said, 'I know not.'

¹³They brought to the Pharisees him that aforetime was blind. ¹⁴And it was the sabbath day when Jesus made the clay, and opened his eyes. ¹⁵Then again the Pharisees also asked him how he had received his sight. He said unto them, 'He put clay upon mine eyes, and I washed, and do see.' ¹⁶Therefore said some of the Pharisees, 'This man is not of God, because he keepeth not the sabbath day.' Others said, 'How

can a man that is a sinner do such miracles?' And there was a division among them. [17] They say unto the blind man again, 'What sayest thou of him, that he hath opened thine eyes?' He said, 'He is a prophet.' [18] But the Jews did not believe concerning him, that he had been blind, and received his sight, until they called the parents of him that had received his sight. [19] And they asked them, saying, 'Is this your son, who ye say was born blind? How then doth he now see?' [20] His parents answered them and said, 'We know that this is our son, and that he was born blind [21] but by what means he now seeth, we know not; or who hath opened his eyes, we know not. He is of age; ask him: he shall speak for himself.' [22] These words spake his parents, because they feared the Jews: for the Jews had agreed already, that if any man did confess that he was Christ, he should be put out of the synagogue. [23] Therefore said his parents, 'He is of age; ask him.' [24] Then again called they the man that was blind, and said unto him, 'Give God the praise; we know that this man is a sinner.' [25] He answered and said, 'Whether he be a sinner or no, I know not; one thing I know, that, whereas I was blind, now I see.' [26] Then said they to him again, 'What did he to thee? How opened he thine eyes?' [27] He answered them, 'I have told you already, and ye did not hear: wherefore would ye hear it again? Will ye also be his disciples?' [28] Then they reviled him, and said, 'Thou art his disciple; but we are Moses' disciples. [29] We know that God spake unto Moses; as for this fellow, we know not from whence he is.' [30] The man answered and said unto them, 'Why herein is a marvellous thing, that ye know not from whence he is, and yet he hath opened mine eyes. ³¹ Now we know that God heareth not sinners, but if any man be a worshipper of God, and doeth his will, him he heareth. ³² Since the world began was it not heard that any man opened the eyes of one that was born blind. ³³ If this man were not of God, he could do nothing.' ³⁴ They answered and said unto him, 'Thou wast altogether born in sins, and dost thou teach us?' And they cast him out. ³⁵ Jesus heard that they had cast him out; and when he had found him, he said unto him, 'Dost thou believe on the Son of God?' ³⁶ He answered and said, 'Who is he, Lord, that I might believe on him?' ³⁷ And Jesus said unto him, 'Thou hast both seen him, and it is he that talketh with thee.' ³⁸ And he said, 'Lord, I believe.' And he worshipped him.

³⁹ And Jesus said, 'For judgment I am come into this world, that they which see not might see; and that they which see might be made blind.' ⁴⁰ And some of the Pharisees which were with him heard these words, and said unto him, 'Are we blind also?' ⁴¹ Jesus said unto them, 'If ye were blind, ye should have no sin, but now ye say, "We see"; therefore your sin remaineth.'

10 'Verily, verily, I say unto you, he that entereth not by the door into the sheepfold, but climbeth up some other way, the same is a thief and a robber. ² But he that entereth in by the door is the shepherd of the sheep. ³ To him the porter openeth; and the sheep hear his voice, and he calleth his own sheep by name, and leadeth them out. ⁴ And when he putteth forth his own sheep, he goeth before them, and the sheep follow him, for they know his voice. ⁵ And a stranger

will they not follow, but will flee from him, for they know not the voice of strangers.' ⁶ This parable spake Jesus unto them, but they understood not what things they were which he spake unto them. ⁷ Then said Jesus unto them again, 'Verily, verily, I say unto you, I am the door of the sheep. ⁸All that ever came before me are thieves and robbers, but the sheep did not hear them. ⁹ I am the door: by me if any man enter in, he shall be saved, and shall go in and out, and find pasture. ¹⁰ The thief cometh not, but for to steal, and to kill, and to destroy: I am come that they might have life, and that they might have it more abundantly. ¹¹ I am the good shepherd: the good shepherd giveth his life for the sheep. ¹² But he that is an hireling, and not the shepherd, whose own the sheep are not, seeth the wolf coming, and leaveth the sheep, and fleeth, and the wolf catcheth them, and scattereth the sheep. ¹³ The hireling fleeth, because he is an hireling, and careth not for the sheep. ¹⁴ I am the good shepherd, and know my sheep, and am known of mine. ¹⁵As the Father knoweth me, even so know I the Father, and I lay down my life for the sheep. ¹⁶And other sheep I have, which are not of this fold: them also I must bring, and they shall hear my voice; and there shall be one fold: and one shepherd. ¹⁷ Therefore doth my Father love me, because I lay down my life, that I might take it again. ¹⁸ No man taketh it from me, but I lay it down of myself. I have power to lay it down, and I have power to take it again. This commandment have I received of my Father.'

¹⁹ There was a division therefore again among the Jews for these sayings. ²⁰And many of them said, 'He hath a devil, and is mad; why hear ye him?' ²¹ Others said, 'These are not

the words of him that hath a devil. Can a devil open the eyes of the blind?'

²²And it was at Jerusalem the feast of the dedication, and it was winter. ²³And Jesus walked in the temple in Solomon's porch. ²⁴Then came the Jews round about him, and said unto him, 'How long dost thou make us to doubt? If thou be the Christ, tell us plainly.' ²⁵Jesus answered them, 'I told you, and ye believed not: the works that I do in my Father's name, they bear witness of me. ²⁶But ye believe not, because ye are not of my sheep, as I said unto you. ²⁷My sheep hear my voice, and I know them, and they follow me, ²⁸and I give unto them eternal life; and they shall never perish, neither shall any man pluck them out of my hand. ²⁹My Father, which gave them me, is greater than all; and no man is able to pluck them out of my Father's hand. ³⁰I and my Father are one.' ³¹Then the Jews took up stones again to stone him. ³²Jesus answered them, 'Many good works have I shewed you from my Father; for which of those works do ye stone me?' ³³The Jews answered him, saying, 'For a good work we stone thee not; but for blasphemy; and because that thou, being a man, makest thyself God.' ³⁴Jesus answered them, 'Is it not written in your law, "I said, ye are gods"? ³⁵If he called them gods, unto whom the word of God came, and the scripture cannot be broken; ³⁶say ye of him, whom the Father hath sanctified, and sent into the world, "Thou blasphemest," because I said, "I am the Son of God"? ³⁷If I do not the works of my Father, believe me not. ³⁸But if I do, though ye believe not me, believe the works: that ye may know, and believe, that the Father is in me, and I in him.' ³⁹Therefore they sought again to take

him: but he escaped out of their hand, [40] and went away again beyond Jordan into the place where John at first baptized; and there he abode. [41]And many resorted unto him, and said, 'John did no miracle, but all things that John spake of this man were true.' [42]And many believed on him there.

11 Now a certain man was sick, named Lazarus, of Bethany, the town of Mary and her sister Martha. [2](It was that Mary which anointed the Lord with ointment, and wiped his feet with her hair, whose brother Lazarus was sick.) [3]Therefore his sisters sent unto him, saying, 'Lord, behold, he whom thou lovest is sick.' [4]When Jesus heard that, he said, 'This sickness is not unto death, but for the glory of God, that the Son of God might be glorified thereby.' [5]Now Jesus loved Martha, and her sister, and Lazarus. [6]When he had heard therefore that he was sick, he abode two days still in the same place where he was. [7]Then after that saith he to his disciples, 'Let us go into Judæa again.' [8]His disciples say unto him, 'Master, the Jews of late sought to stone thee; and goest thou thither again?' [9]Jesus answered, 'Are there not twelve hours in the day? If any man walk in the day, he stumbleth not, because he seeth the light of this world. [10]But if a man walk in the night, he stumbleth, because there is no light in him.' [11]These things said he, and after that he saith unto them, 'Our friend Lazarus sleepeth; but I go, that I may awake him out of sleep.' [12]Then said his disciples, 'Lord, if he sleep, he shall do well.' [13]Howbeit Jesus spake of his death, but they thought that he had spoken of taking of rest in sleep. [14]Then said Jesus unto them plainly, 'Lazarus is dead. [15]And I am

glad for your sakes that I was not there, to the intent ye may believe; nevertheless let us go unto him.' ¹⁶ Then said Thomas, which is called Didymus, unto his fellowdisciples, 'Let us also go, that we may die with him.' ¹⁷ Then when Jesus came, he found that he had lain in the grave four days already. ¹⁸ Now Bethany was nigh unto Jerusalem, about fifteen furlongs off, ¹⁹ and many of the Jews came to Martha and Mary, to comfort them concerning their brother. ²⁰ Then Martha, as soon as she heard that Jesus was coming, went and met him, but Mary sat still in the house. ²¹ Then said Martha unto Jesus, 'Lord, if thou hadst been here, my brother had not died. ²² But I know, that even now, whatsoever thou wilt ask of God, God will give it thee.' ²³ Jesus saith unto her, 'Thy brother shall rise again.' ²⁴ Martha saith unto him, 'I know that he shall rise again in the resurrection at the last day.' ²⁵ Jesus said unto her, 'I am the resurrection, and the life: he that believeth in me, though he were dead, yet shall he live, ²⁶ and whosoever liveth and believeth in me shall never die. Believest thou this?' ²⁷ She saith unto him, 'Yea, Lord, I believe that thou art the Christ, the Son of God, which should come into the world.' ²⁸ And when she had so said, she went her way, and called Mary her sister secretly, saying, 'The Master is come, and calleth for thee.' ²⁹ As soon as she heard that, she arose quickly, and came unto him. ³⁰ Now Jesus was not yet come into the town, but was in that place where Martha met him. ³¹ The Jews then which were with her in the house, and comforted her, when they saw Mary, that she rose up hastily and went out, followed her, saying, 'She goeth unto the grave to weep there.' ³² Then when Mary was come where Jesus was, and saw him, she fell down at his feet, saying unto him, 'Lord, if thou hadst been here, my brother had not died.' ³³ When Jesus therefore saw her weeping, and the Jews also weeping which came with her, he groaned in the spirit, and was troubled, ³⁴ and said, 'Where have ye laid him?' They said unto him, 'Lord, come and see.' ³⁵ Jesus wept. ³⁶ Then said the Jews, 'Behold how he loved him!' ³⁷ And some of them said, 'Could not this man, which opened the eyes of the blind, have caused that even this man should not have died?' ³⁸ Jesus therefore again groaning in himself cometh to the grave. It was a cave, and a stone lay upon it. ³⁹ Jesus said, 'Take ye away the stone.' Martha, the sister of him that was dead, saith unto him, 'Lord, by this time he stinketh, for he hath been dead four days.' ⁴⁰ Jesus saith unto her, 'Said I not unto thee, that, if thou wouldest believe, thou shouldest see the glory of God?' ⁴¹ Then they took away the stone from the place where the dead was laid. And Jesus lifted up his eyes, and said, 'Father, I thank thee that thou hast heard me. ⁴² And I knew that thou hearest me always, but because of the people which stand by I said it, that they may believe that thou hast sent me.' ⁴³ And when he thus had spoken, he cried with a loud voice, 'Lazarus, come forth.' ⁴⁴ And he that was dead came forth, bound hand and foot with graveclothes, and his face was bound about with a napkin. Jesus saith unto them, 'Loose him, and let him go.' ⁴⁵ Then many of the Jews which came to Mary, and had seen the things which Jesus did, believed on him. ⁴⁶ But some of them went their ways to the Pharisees, and told them what things Jesus had done.

⁴⁷ Then gathered the chief priests and the Pharisees a

council, and said, 'What do we? For this man doeth many miracles. ⁴⁸ If we let him thus alone, all men will believe on him, and the Romans shall come and take away both our place and nation.' ⁴⁹ And one of them, named Caiaphas, being the high priest that same year, said unto them, 'Ye know nothing at all, ⁵⁰ nor consider that it is expedient for us, that one man should die for the people, and that the whole nation perish not.' ⁵¹ And this spake he not of himself, but being high priest that year, he prophesied that Jesus should die for that nation; ⁵² and not for that nation only, but that also he should gather together in one the children of God that were scattered abroad. ⁵³ Then from that day forth they took counsel together for to put him to death. ⁵⁴ Jesus therefore walked no more openly among the Jews; but went thence unto a country near to the wilderness, into a city called Ephraim, and there continued with his disciples.

⁵⁵ And the Jews' passover was nigh at hand, and many went out of the country up to Jerusalem before the passover, to purify themselves. ⁵⁶ Then sought they for Jesus, and spake among themselves, as they stood in the temple, 'What think ye, that he will not come to the feast?' ⁵⁷ Now both the chief priests and the Pharisees had given a commandment, that, if any man knew where he were, he should shew it, that they might take him.

12 Then Jesus six days before the passover came to Bethany, where Lazarus was which had been dead, whom he raised from the dead. ² There they made him a supper, and Martha served, but Lazarus was one of them that sat at

the table with him. ³ Then took Mary a pound of ointment of spikenard, very costly, and anointed the feet of Jesus, and wiped his feet with her hair, and the house was filled with the odour of the ointment. ⁴ Then saith one of his disciples, Judas Iscariot, Simon's son, which should betray him, ⁵ 'Why was not this ointment sold for three hundred pence, and given to the poor?' ⁶ This he said, not that he cared for the poor; but because he was a thief, and had the bag, and bare what was put therein. ⁷ Then said Jesus, 'Let her alone: against the day of my burying hath she kept this. ⁸ For the poor always ye have with you; but me ye have not always.' ⁹ Much people of the Jews therefore knew that he was there, and they came not for Jesus' sake only, but that they might see Lazarus also, whom he had raised from the dead.

¹⁰ But the chief priests consulted that they might put Lazarus also to death; ¹¹ because that by reason of him many of the Jews went away, and believed on Jesus.

¹² On the next day much people that were come to the feast, when they heard that Jesus was coming to Jerusalem, ¹³ took branches of palm trees, and went forth to meet him, and cried, 'Hosanna: blessed is the King of Israel that cometh in the name of the Lord.' ¹⁴ And Jesus, when he had found a young ass, sat thereon; as it is written, ¹⁵ 'Fear not, daughter of Sion: behold, thy King cometh, sitting on an ass's colt.' ¹⁶ These things understood not his disciples at the first, but when Jesus was glorified, then remembered they that these things were written of him, and that they had done these things unto him. ¹⁷ The people therefore that was with him when he called Lazarus out of his grave, and raised him from

the dead, bare record. ¹⁸ For this cause the people also met him, for that they heard that he had done this miracle. ¹⁹ The Pharisees therefore said among themselves, 'Perceive ye how ye prevail nothing? Behold, the world is gone after him.'

²⁰ And there were certain Greeks among them that came up to worship at the feast. ²¹ The same came therefore to Philip, which was of Bethsaida of Galilee, and desired him, saying, 'Sir, we would see Jesus.' ²² Philip cometh and telleth Andrew, and again Andrew and Philip tell Jesus.

²³ And Jesus answered them, saying, 'The hour is come, that the Son of man should be glorified. ²⁴ Verily, verily, I say unto you, except a corn of wheat fall into the ground and die, it abideth alone, but if it die, it bringeth forth much fruit. ²⁵ He that loveth his life shall lose it; and he that hateth his life in this world shall keep it unto life eternal. ²⁶ If any man serve me, let him follow me; and where I am, there shall also my servant be: if any man serve me, him will my Father honour. ²⁷ Now is my soul troubled; and what shall I say? "Father, save me from this hour." But for this cause came I unto this hour. ²⁸ Father, glorify thy name.' Then came there a voice from heaven, saying, 'I have both glorified it, and will glorify it again.' ²⁹ The people therefore, that stood by, and heard it, said that it thundered; others said, 'An angel spake to him.' ³⁰ Jesus answered and said, 'This voice came not because of me, but for your sakes. ³¹ Now is the judgment of this world: now shall the prince of this world be cast out. ³² And I, if I be lifted up from the earth, will draw all men unto me.' ³³ This he said, signifying what death he should die. ³⁴ The people answered him, 'We have heard out of the law that

Christ abideth for ever, and how sayest thou the Son of man must be lifted up? Who is this Son of man?' ³⁵ Then Jesus said unto them, 'Yet a little while is the light with you. Walk while ye have the light, lest darkness come upon you: for he that walketh in darkness knoweth not whither he goeth. ³⁶ While ye have light, believe in the light, that ye may be the children of light.' These things spake Jesus, and departed, and did hide himself from them.

³⁷ But though he had done so many miracles before them, yet they believed not on him, ³⁸ that the saying of Esaias the prophet might be fulfilled, which he spake, 'Lord, who hath believed our report? And to whom hath the arm of the Lord been revealed?' ³⁹ Therefore they could not believe, because that Esaias said again, ⁴⁰ 'He hath blinded their eyes, and hardened their heart; that they should not see with their eyes, nor understand with their heart, and be converted, and I should heal them.' ⁴¹ These things said Esaias, when he saw his glory, and spake of him.

⁴² Nevertheless among the chief rulers also many believed on him; but because of the Pharisees they did not confess him, lest they should be put out of the synagogue, ⁴³ for they loved the praise of men more than the praise of God.

⁴⁴ Jesus cried and said, 'He that believeth on me, believeth not on me, but on him that sent me. ⁴⁵ And he that seeth me seeth him that sent me. ⁴⁶ I am come a light into the world, that whosoever believeth on me should not abide in darkness. ⁴⁷ And if any man hear my words, and believe not, I judge him not: for I came not to judge the world, but to save the world. ⁴⁸ He that rejecteth me, and receiveth not my

words, hath one that judgeth him: the word that I have spoken, the same shall judge him in the last day. ⁴⁹ For I have not spoken of myself; but the Father which sent me, he gave me a commandment, what I should say, and what I should speak. ⁵⁰And I know that his commandment is life everlasting: whatsoever I speak therefore, even as the Father said unto me, so I speak.'

13 Now before the feast of the passover, when Jesus knew that his hour was come that he should depart out of this world unto the Father, having loved his own which were in the world, he loved them unto the end. ²And supper being ended, the devil having now put into the heart of Judas Iscariot, Simon's son, to betray him; ³Jesus knowing that the Father had given all things into his hands, and that he was come from God, and went to God; ⁴he riseth from supper, and laid aside his garments; and took a towel, and girded himself. ⁵After that he poureth water into a bason, and began to wash the disciples' feet, and to wipe them with the towel wherewith he was girded. ⁶Then cometh he to Simon Peter, and Peter saith unto him, 'Lord, dost thou wash my feet?' ⁷Jesus answered and said unto him, 'What I do thou knowest not now; but thou shalt know hereafter.' ⁸Peter saith unto him, 'Thou shalt never wash my feet.' Jesus answered him, 'If I wash thee not, thou hast no part with me.' ⁹Simon Peter saith unto him, 'Lord, not my feet only, but also my hands and my head.' ¹⁰Jesus saith to him, 'He that is washed needeth not save to wash his feet, but is clean every whit: and ye are clean, but not all.' ¹¹For he knew who should betray

him; therefore said he, 'Ye are not all clean.' ¹²So after he had washed their feet, and had taken his garments, and was set down again, he said unto them, 'Know ye what I have done to you? ¹³Ye call me "Master" and "Lord", and ye say well; for so I am. ¹⁴If I then, your Lord and Master, have washed your feet, ye also ought to wash one another's feet. ¹⁵For I have given you an example, that ye should do as I have done to you. ¹⁶Verily, verily, I say unto you, the servant is not greater than his lord; neither he that is sent greater than he that sent him. ¹⁷If ye know these things, happy are ye if ye do them.

¹⁸'I speak not of you all; I know whom I have chosen: but that the scripture may be fulfilled. He that eateth bread with me hath lifted up his heel against me. ¹⁹Now I tell you before it come, that, when it is come to pass, ye may believe that I am he. ²⁰Verily, verily, I say unto you, he that receiveth whomsoever I send receiveth me; and he that receiveth me receiveth him that sent me.' ²¹When Jesus had thus said, he was troubled in spirit, and testified, and said, 'Verily, verily, I say unto you, that one of you shall betray me.' ²²Then the disciples looked one on another, doubting of whom he spake. ²³Now there was leaning on Jesus' bosom one of his disciples, whom Jesus loved. ²⁴Simon Peter therefore beckoned to him, that he should ask who it should be of whom he spake. ²⁵He then lying on Jesus' breast saith unto him, 'Lord, who is it?' ²⁶Jesus answered, 'He it is, to whom I shall give a sop, when I have dipped it.' And when he had dipped the sop, he gave it to Judas Iscariot, the son of Simon. ²⁷And after the sop Satan entered into him. Then said Jesus unto him, 'That thou doest, do quickly.' ²⁸Now no man at the table

knew for what intent he spake this unto him. ²⁹ For some of them thought, because Judas had the bag, that Jesus had said unto him, 'Buy those things that we have need of against the feast,' or, that he should give something to the poor. ³⁰ He then having received the sop went immediately out, and it was night.

³¹ Therefore, when he was gone out, Jesus said, 'Now is the Son of man glorified, and God is glorified in him. ³² If God be glorified in him, God shall also glorify him in himself, and shall straightway glorify him. ³³ Little children, yet a little while I am with you. Ye shall seek me, and as I said unto the Jews, "Whither I go, ye cannot come"; so now I say to you. ³⁴ A new commandment I give unto you, that ye love one another; as I have loved you, that ye also love one another. ³⁵ By this shall all men know that ye are my disciples, if ye have love one to another.'

³⁶ Simon Peter said unto him, 'Lord, whither goest thou?' Jesus answered him, 'Whither I go, thou canst not follow me now; but thou shalt follow me afterwards.' ³⁷ Peter said unto him, 'Lord, why cannot I follow thee now? I will lay down my life for thy sake.' ³⁸ Jesus answered him, 'Wilt thou lay down thy life for my sake? Verily, verily, I say unto thee, the cock shall not crow, till thou hast denied me thrice.

14 'Let not your heart be troubled: ye believe in God, believe also in me. ² In my Father's house are many mansions: if it were not so, I would have told you. I go to prepare a place for you. ³ And if I go and prepare a place for you, I will come again, and receive you unto myself; that

where I am, there ye may be also. ⁴And whither I go ye know, and the way ye know.' ⁵Thomas saith unto him, 'Lord, we know not whither thou goest; and how can we know the way?' ⁶Jesus saith unto him, 'I am the way, the truth, and the life: no man cometh unto the Father, but by me. ⁷If ye had known me, ye should have known my Father also: and from henceforth ye know him, and have seen him.' ⁸Philip saith unto him, 'Lord, shew us the Father, and it sufficeth us.' ⁹Jesus saith unto him, 'Have I been so long time with you, and yet hast thou not known me, Philip? He that hath seen me hath seen the Father; and how sayest thou then, "Shew us the Father"? ¹⁰Believest thou not that I am in the Father, and the Father in me? The words that I speak unto you I speak not of myself; but the Father that dwelleth in me, he doeth the works. ¹¹Believe me that I am in the Father, and the Father in me, or else believe me for the very works' sake. ¹²Verily, verily, I say unto you, he that believeth on me, the works that I do shall he do also; and greater works than these shall he do; because I go unto my Father. ¹³And whatsoever ye shall ask in my name, that will I do, that the Father may be glorified in the Son. ¹⁴If ye shall ask any thing in my name, I will do it.

¹⁵'If ye love me, keep my commandments. ¹⁶And I will pray the Father, and he shall give you another Comforter, that he may abide with you for ever; ¹⁷even the Spirit of truth; whom the world cannot receive, because it seeth him not, neither knoweth him, but ye know him; for he dwelleth with you, and shall be in you. ¹⁸I will not leave you comfortless; I will come to you. ¹⁹Yet a little while, and the world seeth me no more; but ye see me: because I live, ye shall live

also. ²⁰At that day ye shall know that I am in my Father, and ye in me, and I in you. ²¹He that hath my commandments, and keepeth them, he it is that loveth me: and he that loveth me shall be loved of my Father, and I will love him, and will manifest myself to him.' ²²Judas saith unto him, not Iscariot, 'Lord, how is it that thou wilt manifest thyself unto us, and not unto the world?' ²³Jesus answered and said unto him, 'If a man love me, he will keep my words: and my Father will love him, and we will come unto him, and make our abode with him. ²⁴He that loveth me not keepeth not my sayings, and the word which ye hear is not mine, but the Father's which sent me. ²⁵These things have I spoken unto you, being yet present with you. ²⁶But the Comforter, which is the Holy Ghost, whom the Father will send in my name, he shall teach you all things, and bring all things to your remembrance, whatsoever I have said unto you. ²⁷Peace I leave with you, my peace I give unto you: not as the world giveth, give I unto you. Let not your heart be troubled, neither let it be afraid. ²⁸Ye have heard how I said unto you, "I go away, and come again unto you." If ye loved me, ye would rejoice, because I said I go unto the Father, for my Father is greater than I. ²⁹And now I have told you before it come to pass, that, when it is come to pass, ye might believe. ³⁰Hereafter I will not talk much with you, for the prince of this world cometh, and hath nothing in me. ³¹But that the world may know that I love the Father; and as the Father gave me commandment, even so I do. Arise, let us go hence.

15 ¹'I am the true vine, and my Father is the husbandman. ²Every branch in me that beareth not fruit he taketh away, and every branch that beareth fruit, he purgeth it, that it may bring forth more fruit. ³Now ye are clean through the word which I have spoken unto you. ⁴Abide in me, and I in you. As the branch cannot bear fruit of itself, except it abide in the vine; no more can ye, except ye abide in me. ⁵I am the vine, ye are the branches. He that abideth in me, and I in him, the same bringeth forth much fruit, for without me ye can do nothing. ⁶If a man abide not in me, he is cast forth as a branch, and is withered; and men gather them, and cast them into the fire, and they are burned. ⁷If ye abide in me, and my words abide in you, ye shall ask what ye will, and it shall be done unto you. ⁸Herein is my Father glorified, that ye bear much fruit; so shall ye be my disciples. ⁹As the Father hath loved me, so have I loved you; continue ye in my love. ¹⁰If ye keep my commandments, ye shall abide in my love; even as I have kept my Father's commandments, and abide in his love. ¹¹These things have I spoken unto you, that my joy might remain in you, and that your joy might be full.

¹²'This is my commandment: that ye love one another, as I have loved you. ¹³Greater love hath no man than this, that a man lay down his life for his friends. ¹⁴Ye are my friends, if ye do whatsoever I command you. ¹⁵Henceforth I call you not servants; for the servant knoweth not what his lord doeth; but I have called you friends, for all things that I have heard of my Father I have made known unto you. ¹⁶Ye have not chosen me, but I have chosen you, and ordained you, that ye should go and bring forth fruit, and that your fruit should

remain: that whatsoever ye shall ask of the Father in my name, he may give it you. ¹⁷ These things I command you, that ye love one another.

¹⁸ 'If the world hate you, ye know that it hated me before it hated you. ¹⁹ If ye were of the world, the world would love his own: but because ye are not of the world, but I have chosen you out of the world, therefore the world hateth you. ²⁰ Remember the word that I said unto you, "The servant is not greater than his lord." If they have persecuted me, they will also persecute you; if they have kept my saying, they will keep yours also. ²¹ But all these things will they do unto you for my name's sake, because they know not him that sent me. ²² If I had not come and spoken unto them, they had not had sin: but now they have no cloke for their sin. ²³ He that hateth me hateth my Father also. ²⁴ If I had not done among them the works which none other man did, they had not had sin: but now have they both seen and hated both me and my Father. ²⁵ But this cometh to pass, that the word might be fulfilled that is written in their law: "They hated me without a cause."

²⁶ 'But when the Comforter is come, whom I will send unto you from the Father, even the Spirit of truth, which proceedeth from the Father, he shall testify of me. ²⁷ And ye also shall bear witness, because ye have been with me from the beginning.

16 'These things have I spoken unto you, that ye should not be offended. ² They shall put you out of the synagogues: yea, the time cometh, that whosoever killeth you will think that he doeth God service. ³ And these things will they

do unto you, because they have not known the Father, nor me. [4] But these things have I told you, that when the time shall come, ye may remember that I told you of them. And these things I said not unto you at the beginning, because I was with you. [5] But now I go my way to him that sent me; and none of you asketh me, "Whither goest thou?" [6] But because I have said these things unto you, sorrow hath filled your heart. [7] Nevertheless I tell you the truth. It is expedient for you that I go away: for if I go not away, the Comforter will not come unto you; but if I depart, I will send him unto you. [8] And when he is come, he will reprove the world of sin, and of righteousness, and of judgment: [9] of sin, because they believe not on me; [10] of righteousness, because I go to my Father, and ye see me no more; [11] of judgment, because the prince of this world is judged. [12] I have yet many things to say unto you, but ye cannot bear them now. [13] Howbeit when he, the Spirit of truth, is come, he will guide you into all truth, for he shall not speak of himself; but whatsoever he shall hear, that shall he speak, and he will shew you things to come. [14] He shall glorify me, for he shall receive of mine, and shall shew it unto you. [15] All things that the Father hath are mine: therefore said I, that he shall take of mine, and shall shew it unto you.

[16] 'A little while, and ye shall not see me, and again, a little while, and ye shall see me, because I go to the Father.' [17] Then said some of his disciples among themselves, 'What is this that he saith unto us, "A little while, and ye shall not see me, and again, a little while, and ye shall see me," and, "Because I go to the Father"?' [18] They said therefore, 'What is this that he saith, "A little while?" We cannot tell what he

saith.' ¹⁹ Now Jesus knew that they were desirous to ask him, and said unto them, 'Do ye enquire among yourselves of that I said, "A little while, and ye shall not see me, and again, a little while, and ye shall see me"? ²⁰ Verily, verily, I say unto you that ye shall weep and lament, but the world shall rejoice; and ye shall be sorrowful, but your sorrow shall be turned into joy. ²¹ A woman when she is in travail hath sorrow, because her hour is come, but as soon as she is delivered of the child, she remembereth no more the anguish, for joy that a man is born into the world. ²² And ye now therefore have sorrow, but I will see you again, and your heart shall rejoice, and your joy no man taketh from you. ²³ And in that day ye shall ask me nothing. Verily, verily, I say unto you, whatsoever ye shall ask the Father in my name, he will give it you. ²⁴ Hitherto have ye asked nothing in my name: ask, and ye shall receive, that your joy may be full.

²⁵ 'These things have I spoken unto you in proverbs, but the time cometh, when I shall no more speak unto you in proverbs, but I shall shew you plainly of the Father. ²⁶ At that day ye shall ask in my name, and I say not unto you that I will pray the Father for you, ²⁷ for the Father himself loveth you, because ye have loved me, and have believed that I came out from God. ²⁸ I came forth from the Father, and am come into the world; again, I leave the world, and go to the Father.'

²⁹ His disciples said unto him, 'Lo, now speakest thou plainly, and speakest no proverb. ³⁰ Now are we sure that thou knowest all things, and needest not that any man should ask thee: by this we believe that thou camest forth from God.' ³¹ Jesus answered them, 'Do ye now believe? ³² Behold, the

hour cometh, yea, is now come, that ye shall be scattered, every man to his own, and shall leave me alone, and yet I am not alone; because the Father is with me. ³³ These things I have spoken unto you, that in me ye might have peace. In the world ye shall have tribulation: but be of good cheer; I have overcome the world.'

17 These words spake Jesus, and lifted up his eyes to heaven, and said, 'Father, the hour is come; glorify thy Son, that thy Son also may glorify thee. ²As thou hast given him power over all flesh, that he should give eternal life to as many as thou hast given him. ³And this is life eternal, that they might know thee the only true God, and Jesus Christ, whom thou hast sent. ⁴I have glorified thee on the earth: I have finished the work which thou gavest me to do. ⁵And now, O Father, glorify thou me with thine own self with the glory which I had with thee before the world was.

⁶ 'I have manifested thy name unto the men which thou gavest me out of the world: thine they were, and thou gavest them me; and they have kept thy word. ⁷Now they have known that all things whatsoever thou hast given me are of thee. ⁸For I have given unto them the words which thou gavest me; and they have received them, and have known surely that I came out from thee, and they have believed that thou didst send me. ⁹I pray for them: I pray not for the world, but for them which thou hast given me; for they are thine. ¹⁰And all mine are thine, and thine are mine; and I am glorified in them. ¹¹And now I am no more in the world, but these are in the world, and I come to thee. Holy Father, keep

through thine own name those whom thou hast given me, that they may be one, as we are. ¹²While I was with them in the world, I kept them in thy name; those that thou gavest me I have kept, and none of them is lost, but the son of perdition; that the scripture might be fulfilled. ¹³And now come I to thee; and these things I speak in the world, that they might have my joy fulfilled in themselves. ¹⁴I have given them thy word; and the world hath hated them, because they are not of the world, even as I am not of the world. ¹⁵I pray not that thou shouldest take them out of the world, but that thou shouldest keep them from the evil. ¹⁶They are not of the world, even as I am not of the world. ¹⁷Sanctify them through thy truth: thy word is truth. ¹⁸As thou hast sent me into the world, even so have I also sent them into the world. ¹⁹And for their sakes I sanctify myself, that they also might be sanctified through the truth.

²⁰'Neither pray I for these alone, but for them also which shall believe on me through their word; ²¹that they all may be one; as thou, Father, art in me, and I in thee, that they also may be one in us: that the world may believe that thou hast sent me. ²²And the glory which thou gavest me I have given them; that they may be one, even as we are one: ²³I in them, and thou in me, that they may be made perfect in one; and that the world may know that thou hast sent me, and hast loved them, as thou hast loved me. ²⁴Father, I will that they also, whom thou hast given me, be with me where I am; that they may behold my glory, which thou hast given me, for thou lovedst me before the foundation of the world.

²⁵'O righteous Father, the world hath not known thee,

but I have known thee, and these have known that thou hast sent me. ²⁶And I have declared unto them thy name, and will declare it, that the love wherewith thou hast loved me may be in them, and I in them.'

18 When Jesus had spoken these words, he went forth with his disciples over the brook Cedron, where was a garden, into the which he entered, and his disciples. ²And Judas also, which betrayed him, knew the place, for Jesus ofttimes resorted thither with his disciples. ³Judas then, having received a band of men and officers from the chief priests and Pharisees, cometh thither with lanterns and torches and weapons. ⁴Jesus therefore, knowing all things that should come upon him, went forth, and said unto them, 'Whom seek ye?' ⁵They answered him, 'Jesus of Nazareth.' Jesus saith unto them, 'I am he.' And Judas also, which betrayed him, stood with them. ⁶As soon then as he had said unto them, 'I am he,' they went backward, and fell to the ground. ⁷Then asked he them again, 'Whom seek ye?' And they said, 'Jesus of Nazareth.' ⁸Jesus answered, 'I have told you that I am he: if therefore ye seek me, let these go their way,' ⁹that the saying might be fulfilled, which he spake: 'Of them which thou gavest me have I lost none.' ¹⁰Then Simon Peter having a sword drew it, and smote the high priest's servant, and cut off his right ear. The servant's name was Malchus. ¹¹Then said Jesus unto Peter, 'Put up thy sword into the sheath; the cup which my Father hath given me, shall I not drink it?' ¹²Then the band and the captain and officers of the Jews took Jesus, and bound him, ¹³and led him away to Annas first; for

he was father-in-law to Caiaphas, which was the high priest that same year. ¹⁴Now Caiaphas was he, which gave counsel to the Jews, that it was expedient that one man should die for the people.

¹⁵And Simon Peter followed Jesus, and so did another disciple; that disciple was known unto the high priest, and went in with Jesus into the palace of the high priest. ¹⁶But Peter stood at the door without. Then went out that other disciple, which was known unto the high priest, and spake unto her that kept the door, and brought in Peter. ¹⁷Then saith the damsel that kept the door unto Peter, 'Art not thou also one of this man's disciples?' He saith, 'I am not.' ¹⁸And the servants and officers stood there, who had made a fire of coals, for it was cold, and they warmed themselves, and Peter stood with them, and warmed himself.

¹⁹The high priest then asked Jesus of his disciples, and of his doctrine. ²⁰Jesus answered him, 'I spake openly to the world; I ever taught in the synagogue, and in the temple, whither the Jews always resort; and in secret have I said nothing. ²¹Why askest thou me? Ask them which heard me, what I have said unto them; behold, they know what I said.' ²²And when he had thus spoken, one of the officers which stood by struck Jesus with the palm of his hand, saying, 'Answerest thou the high priest so?' ²³Jesus answered him, 'If I have spoken evil, bear witness of the evil, but if well, why smitest thou me?' ²⁴Now Annas had sent him bound unto Caiaphas the high priest. ²⁵And Simon Peter stood and warmed himself. They said therefore unto him, 'Art not thou also one of his disciples?' He denied it, and said, 'I am not.'

²⁶ One of the servants of the high priest, being his kinsman whose ear Peter cut off, saith, 'Did not I see thee in the garden with him?' ²⁷ Peter then denied again, and immediately the cock crew.

²⁸ Then led they Jesus from Caiaphas unto the hall of judgment, and it was early; and they themselves went not into the judgment hall, lest they should be defiled; but that they might eat the passover. ²⁹ Pilate then went out unto them, and said, 'What accusation bring ye against this man?' ³⁰ They answered and said unto him, 'If he were not a malefactor, we would not have delivered him up unto thee.' ³¹ Then said Pilate unto them, 'Take ye him, and judge him according to your law.' The Jews therefore said unto him, 'It is not lawful for us to put any man to death,' ³² that the saying of Jesus might be fulfilled, which he spake, signifying what death he should die. ³³ Then Pilate entered into the judgment hall again, and called Jesus, and said unto him, 'Art thou the King of the Jews?' ³⁴ Jesus answered him, 'Sayest thou this thing of thyself, or did others tell it thee of me?' ³⁵ Pilate answered, 'Am I a Jew? Thine own nation and the chief priests have delivered thee unto me; what hast thou done?' ³⁶ Jesus answered, 'My kingdom is not of this world: if my kingdom were of this world, then would my servants fight, that I should not be delivered to the Jews, but now is my kingdom not from hence.' ³⁷ Pilate therefore said unto him, 'Art thou a king then?' Jesus answered, 'Thou sayest that I am a king. To this end was I born, and for this cause came I into the world, that I should bear witness unto the truth. Every one that is of the truth heareth my voice.' ³⁸ Pilate saith unto him, 'What is

truth?' And when he had said this, he went out again unto the Jews, and saith unto them, 'I find in him no fault at all. ³⁹ But ye have a custom, that I should release unto you one at the passover: will ye therefore that I release unto you the King of the Jews?' ⁴⁰ Then cried they all again, saying, 'Not this man, but Barabbas.' Now Barabbas was a robber.

19 Then Pilate therefore took Jesus, and scourged him. ²And the soldiers platted a crown of thorns, and put it on his head, and they put on him a purple robe, ³and said, 'Hail, King of the Jews!' and they smote him with their hands. ⁴Pilate therefore went forth again, and saith unto them, 'Behold, I bring him forth to you, that ye may know that I find no fault in him.' ⁵Then came Jesus forth, wearing the crown of thorns, and the purple robe. And Pilate saith unto them, 'Behold the man!' ⁶When the chief priests therefore and officers saw him, they cried out, saying, 'Crucify him, crucify him.' Pilate saith unto them, 'Take ye him, and crucify him, for I find no fault in him.' ⁷The Jews answered him, 'We have a law, and by our law he ought to die, because he made himself the Son of God.'

⁸When Pilate therefore heard that saying, he was the more afraid, ⁹and went again into the judgment hall, and saith unto Jesus, 'Whence art thou?' But Jesus gave him no answer. ¹⁰Then saith Pilate unto him, 'Speakest thou not unto me? Knowest thou not that I have power to crucify thee, and have power to release thee?' ¹¹Jesus answered, 'Thou couldest have no power at all against me, except it were given thee from above: therefore he that delivered me unto thee

hath the greater sin.' ¹²And from thenceforth Pilate sought to release him, but the Jews cried out, saying, 'If thou let this man go, thou art not Cæsar's friend; whosoever maketh himself a king speaketh against Cæsar.'

¹³ When Pilate therefore heard that saying, he brought Jesus forth, and sat down in the judgment seat in a place that is called the Pavement, but in the Hebrew, Gabbatha. ¹⁴And it was the preparation of the passover, and about the sixth hour, and he saith unto the Jews, 'Behold your King!' ¹⁵ But they cried out, 'Away with him, away with him, crucify him.' Pilate saith unto them, 'Shall I crucify your King?' The chief priests answered, 'We have no king but Cæsar.' ¹⁶ Then delivered he him therefore unto them to be crucified. And they took Jesus, and led him away. ¹⁷And he bearing his cross went forth into a place called the place of a skull, which is called in the Hebrew Golgotha, ¹⁸ where they crucified him, and two other with him, on either side one, and Jesus in the midst.

¹⁹And Pilate wrote a title, and put it on the cross. And the writing was, 'Jesus of Nazareth the King of the Jews.' ²⁰ This title then read many of the Jews, for the place where Jesus was crucified was nigh to the city, and it was written in Hebrew, and Greek, and Latin. ²¹ Then said the chief priests of the Jews to Pilate, 'Write not, "The King of the Jews", but that he said, "I am King of the Jews."' ²² Pilate answered, 'What I have written I have written.'

²³ Then the soldiers, when they had crucified Jesus, took his garments, and made four parts, to every soldier a part; and also his coat. Now the coat was without seam, woven from the top throughout. ²⁴ They said therefore among themselves,

'Let us not rend it, but cast lots for it, whose it shall be,' that the scripture might be fulfilled, which saith, 'They parted my raiment among them, and for my vesture they did cast lots.' These things therefore the soldiers did.

²⁵ Now there stood by the cross of Jesus his mother, and his mother's sister, Mary the wife of Cleophas, and Mary Magdalene. ²⁶ When Jesus therefore saw his mother, and the disciple standing by, whom he loved, he saith unto his mother, 'Woman, behold thy son!' ²⁷ Then saith he to the disciple, 'Behold thy mother!' And from that hour that disciple took her unto his own home.

²⁸ After this, Jesus knowing that all things were now accomplished, that the scripture might be fulfilled, saith, 'I thirst.' ²⁹ Now there was set a vessel full of vinegar, and they filled a spunge with vinegar, and put it upon hyssop, and put it to his mouth. ³⁰ When Jesus therefore had received the vinegar, he said, 'It is finished,' and he bowed his head, and gave up the ghost. ³¹ The Jews therefore, because it was the preparation, that the bodies should not remain upon the cross on the sabbath day (for that sabbath day was an high day), besought Pilate that their legs might be broken, and that they might be taken away. ³² Then came the soldiers, and brake the legs of the first, and of the other which was crucified with him. ³³ But when they came to Jesus, and saw that he was dead already, they brake not his legs, ³⁴ but one of the soldiers with a spear pierced his side, and forthwith came there out blood and water. ³⁵ And he that saw it bare record, and his record is true, and he knoweth that he saith true, that ye might believe. ³⁶ For these things were done,

that the scripture should be fulfilled: 'A bone of him shall not be broken.' ³⁷And again another scripture saith, 'They shall look on him whom they pierced.'

³⁸And after this Joseph of Arimathæa, being a disciple of Jesus, but secretly for fear of the Jews, besought Pilate that he might take away the body of Jesus, and Pilate gave him leave. He came therefore, and took the body of Jesus. ³⁹And there came also Nicodemus, which at the first came to Jesus by night, and brought a mixture of myrrh and aloes, about an hundred pound weight. ⁴⁰Then took they the body of Jesus, and wound it in linen clothes with the spices, as the manner of the Jews is to bury. ⁴¹Now in the place where he was crucified there was a garden; and in the garden a new sepulchre, wherein was never man yet laid. ⁴²There laid they Jesus therefore because of the Jews' preparation day, for the sepulchre was nigh at hand.

20 The first day of the week cometh Mary Magdalene early, when it was yet dark, unto the sepulchre, and seeth the stone taken away from the sepulchre. ²Then she runneth, and cometh to Simon Peter, and to the other disciple, whom Jesus loved, and saith unto them, 'They have taken away the Lord out of the sepulchre, and we know not where they have laid him.' ³Peter therefore went forth, and that other disciple, and came to the sepulchre. ⁴So they ran both together, and the other disciple did outrun Peter, and came first to the sepulchre. ⁵And he stooping down, and looking in, saw the linen clothes lying; yet went he not in. ⁶Then cometh Simon Peter following him, and went into the sepulchre, and seeth

the linen clothes lie, ⁷and the napkin, that was about his head, not lying with the linen clothes, but wrapped together in a place by itself. ⁸Then went in also that other disciple, which came first to the sepulchre, and he saw, and believed. ⁹For as yet they knew not the scripture, that he must rise again from the dead. ¹⁰Then the disciples went away again unto their own home.

¹¹But Mary stood without at the sepulchre weeping, and as she wept, she stooped down, and looked into the sepulchre, ¹²and seeth two angels in white sitting, the one at the head, and the other at the feet, where the body of Jesus had lain. ¹³And they say unto her, 'Woman, why weepest thou?' She saith unto them, 'Because they have taken away my Lord, and I know not where they have laid him.' ¹⁴And when she had thus said, she turned herself back, and saw Jesus standing, and knew not that it was Jesus. ¹⁵Jesus saith unto her, 'Woman, why weepest thou? Whom seekest thou?' She, supposing him to be the gardener, saith unto him, 'Sir, if thou have borne him hence, tell me where thou hast laid him, and I will take him away.' ¹⁶Jesus saith unto her, 'Mary.' She turned herself, and saith unto him, 'Rabboni,' which is to say, 'Master'. ¹⁷Jesus saith unto her, 'Touch me not, for I am not yet ascended to my Father, but go to my brethren, and say unto them, "I ascend unto my Father, and your Father; and to my God, and your God."' ¹⁸Mary Magdalene came and told the disciples that she had seen the Lord, and that he had spoken these things unto her.

¹⁹Then the same day at evening, being the first day of the week, when the doors were shut where the disciples were

assembled for fear of the Jews, came Jesus and stood in the midst, and saith unto them, 'Peace be unto you.' [20]And when he had so said, he shewed unto them his hands and his side. Then were the disciples glad, when they saw the Lord. [21]Then said Jesus to them again, 'Peace be unto you: as my Father hath sent me, even so send I you.' [22]And when he had said this, he breathed on them, and saith unto them, 'Receive ye the Holy Ghost. [23]Whose soever sins ye remit, they are remitted unto them; and whose soever sins ye retain, they are retained.'

[24]But Thomas, one of the twelve, called Didymus, was not with them when Jesus came. [25]The other disciples therefore said unto him, 'We have seen the Lord.' But he said unto them, 'Except I shall see in his hands the print of the nails, and put my finger into the print of the nails, and thrust my hand into his side, I will not believe.'

[26]And after eight days again his disciples were within, and Thomas with them; then came Jesus, the doors being shut, and stood in the midst, and said, 'Peace be unto you.' [27]Then saith he to Thomas, 'Reach hither thy finger, and behold my hands; and reach hither thy hand, and thrust it into my side; and be not faithless, but believing.' [28]And Thomas answered and said unto him, 'My Lord and my God.' [29]Jesus saith unto him, 'Thomas, because thou hast seen me, thou hast believed: blessed are they that have not seen, and yet have believed.'

[30]And many other signs truly did Jesus in the presence of his disciples, which are not written in this book: [31]but these are written, that ye might believe that Jesus is the Christ, the Son of God; and that believing ye might have life through his name.

21 After these things Jesus shewed himself again to the disciples at the sea of Tiberias; and on this wise shewed he himself. ²There were together Simon Peter, and Thomas called Didymus, and Nathanael of Cana in Galilee, and the sons of Zebedee, and two other of his disciples. ³Simon Peter saith unto them, 'I go a fishing.' They say unto him, 'We also go with thee.' They went forth, and entered into a ship immediately; and that night they caught nothing. ⁴But when the morning was now come, Jesus stood on the shore, but the disciples knew not that it was Jesus. ⁵Then Jesus saith unto them, 'Children, have ye any meat?' They answered him, 'No.' ⁶And he said unto them, 'Cast the net on the right side of the ship, and ye shall find.' They cast therefore, and now they were not able to draw it for the multitude of fishes. ⁷Therefore that disciple whom Jesus loved saith unto Peter, 'It is the Lord.' Now when Simon Peter heard that it was the Lord, he girt his fisher's coat unto him (for he was naked), and did cast himself into the sea. ⁸And the other disciples came in a little ship (for they were not far from land, but as it were two hundred cubits), dragging the net with fishes. ⁹As soon then as they were come to land, they saw a fire of coals there, and fish laid thereon, and bread. ¹⁰Jesus saith unto them, 'Bring of the fish which ye have now caught.' ¹¹Simon Peter went up, and drew the net to land full of great fishes, an hundred and fifty and three, and for all there were so many, yet was not the net broken. ¹²Jesus saith unto them, 'Come and dine.' And none of the disciples durst ask him, 'Who art thou?' knowing that it was the Lord. ¹³Jesus then cometh, and taketh bread, and giveth them, and fish

likewise. ¹⁴ This is now the third time that Jesus shewed himself to his disciples, after that he was risen from the dead.

¹⁵ So when they had dined, Jesus saith to Simon Peter, 'Simon, son of Jonas, lovest thou me more than these?' He saith unto him, 'Yea, Lord; thou knowest that I love thee.' He saith unto him, 'Feed my lambs.' ¹⁶ He saith to him again the second time, 'Simon, son of Jonas, lovest thou me?' He saith unto him, 'Yea, Lord; thou knowest that I love thee.' He saith unto him, 'Feed my sheep.' ¹⁷ He saith unto him the third time, 'Simon, son of Jonas, lovest thou me?' Peter was grieved because he said unto him the third time, 'Lovest thou me?' And he said unto him, 'Lord, thou knowest all things; thou knowest that I love thee.' Jesus saith unto him, 'Feed my sheep.' ¹⁸ Verily, verily, I say unto thee, 'When thou wast young, thou girdedst thyself, and walkedst whither thou wouldest, but when thou shalt be old, thou shalt stretch forth thy hands, and another shall gird thee, and carry thee whither thou wouldest not.' ¹⁹ This spake he, signifying by what death he should glorify God. And when he had spoken this, he saith unto him, 'Follow me.' ²⁰ Then Peter, turning about, seeth the disciple whom Jesus loved following, which also leaned on his breast at supper, and said, 'Lord, which is he that betrayeth thee?' ²¹ Peter seeing him saith to Jesus, 'Lord, and what shall this man do?' ²² Jesus saith unto him, 'If I will that he tarry till I come, what is that to thee? Follow thou me.' ²³ Then went this saying abroad among the brethren, that that disciple should not die; yet Jesus said not unto him, 'He shall not die,' but, 'If I will that he tarry till I come, what is that to thee?' ²⁴ This is the disciple which testifieth of

these things, and wrote these things, and we know that his testimony is true. [25]And there are also many other things which Jesus did, the which, if they should be written every one, I suppose that even the world itself could not contain the books that should be written. Amen.

titles in the series

genesis – *introduced by steven rose*
exodus – *introduced by david grossman*
job – *introduced by louis de bernières*
proverbs – *introduced by charles johnson*
ecclesiastes – *introduced by doris lessing*
song of solomon – *introduced by a s byatt*
matthew – *introduced by a n wilson*
mark – *introduced by nick cave*
luke – *introduced by richard holloway*
john – *introduced by blake morrison*
corinthians – *introduced by fay weldon*
revelation – *introduced by will self*